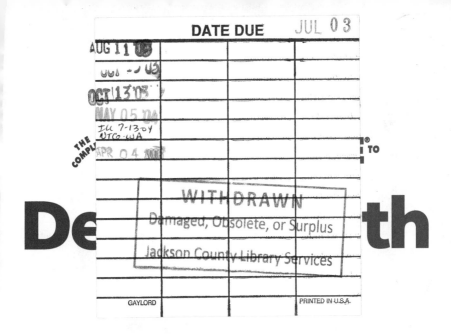

THE COMPL... ® TO

De th

for Teens

by Sa... Vanessa Torres

A
ALPHA
A Pearson Education Company

Copyright © 2002 by Sara Jane Sluke and Vanessa Torres

International Standard Book Number: 0028643011
Library of Congress Catalog Card Number: 2001095861

04   03   02   8   7   6   5   4   3   2   1

Interpretation of the printing code: The rightmost number of the first series of numbers is the year of the book's printing; the rightmost number of the second series of numbers is the number of the book's printing. For example, a printing code of 02-1 shows that the first printing occurred in 2002.

Printed in the United States of America

Publisher: *Marie Butler-Knight*
Product Manager: *Phil Kitchel*
Managing Editor: *Jennifer Chisholm*
Acquisitions Editor: *Randy Ladenheim-Gil*
Development Editor: *Deborah S. Romaine*
Production Editor: *Billy Fields*
Copy Editor: *Krista Hansing*
Illustrator: *Jody P. Schaeffer*
Cover Designer: *Kurt Owens, Trina Wurst*
Book Designer: *Trina Wurst*
Layout/Proofreading: *Angela Calvert, Susan Geiselman, Mary Hunt*

Contents at a Glance

Contents

Introduction

Millennium Teens

Today's teens are coming of age during the dawn of a new millennium. The world is a rapidly changing place that requires everyone to keep up or get lost. Faced with technological advances unique to the information age, a modern teen can feel directionless in a world of choices and options. However, technology hasn't done a thing to revolutionize adolescence, thank you very much. You're still dealing with a slew of physical and emotional changes and the question of whether to start taking more control over your own life.

Stress Distress

All of these elements are impossible to eliminate or ignore, and they'll make for some very challenging roads ahead. Feeling overwhelmed by your developing body, the exciting stirrings of first love, and the amount of stuff that you are expected to accomplish, both personally and academically, over the next few years can make you a prime candidate for burnout.

And that's what we are trying to avoid. Certain stresses in life are unavoidable, and if you don't learn how to deal with them effectively, it can seriously influence your quality of life. The goal here is not to turn you into a superhuman, but to make you feel as normal as possible on a daily basis, not like some freak show spinning out of control. In this book, we'll show you how to gain some control over your life and how to best handle the things that are out of your power.

We Can Work It Out

The Complete Idiot's Guide to Dealing with Stress for Teens is broken up into three sections. They explain and explore stress, and then teach you how to manage it. This is what you're in for.

Part 1, "The Stress Mess": Stress is tough to deal with, and it takes no prisoners. In Chapter 1, "The World Can Be Heavy, Give

Your Shoulders a Rest," we define what stress is and how it makes you feel. Chapter 2, "Growing Up Is Hard to Do," explains how and why it's more stressful to grow up in this day and age than ever before. Like being a teen isn't hard enough! Chapter 3, "The Inside Jive," will check out how you're responsible for creating a lot of the stress you feel. In Chapter 4, "Physically Fit to Be Tied," we'll go over the mind-body connection and how stress can affect you physically.

Part 2, "Pressure, Pressure Everywhere": The stress that is put on you is intense, and at times it feels like it'll never let up. In this section, we'll take a look at the various places stress comes from. In Chapter 5, "School Dazed and Confused," we'll take a walk through your classrooms and hallways, checking out all the different parts of school life that can pile on the pressure. Chapter 6, "Harried at Home," examines how stressed you can get when there's trouble on the home front.

Part 3, "Taming Tension: Fighting the Fire with Force": It's easy to let stress overwhelm you, but you don't have to sit by and let it happen. In this section, we'll teach you how to take control of your own life and refuse to let stress take hold. In Chapter 7, "Finding a Fine Timeline," we'll discuss how difficult it is to balance your days when you're booked solid from morning 'til night. We'll show you how to better manage your time, which will help take some of the heat off. Chapter 8, "Taking It Down a Notch," explains how you can avoid letting your temper get the best of you. Chapter 9, "Be a Control Freak," warns of some traps that can easily rob you of control over your own actions, thoughts, and feelings. Don't worry, we also teach you how you can grab it back. In Chapter 10, "Decisions, Decisions, Decisions," we'll check out some great problem-solving techniques and give advice on how to make sound, educated decisions. In Chapter 11, "Zen and the Art of Attitude Adjustment," we'll give you a bunch of suggestions on how to destress yourself and avoid it in the first place. Chapter 12, "Success Through Stress," shows how stress doesn't have to be a bad thing and can actually work for you.

Tasty Nuggets

Inside this book, you'll find boxes that highlight additional helpful info. Let us explain.

Beware of Burnout

These are warnings to help steer you clear of those nasty stress pitfalls.

Fighting the Funk

Check out these boxes for some handy tips on how to keep yourself from getting steamrolled by stress.

Keepin' It Real

Get the skinny on what other teens are going through and how they handle situations when the heat is on.

Girls vs. Boys

We use "she" and "he" randomly throughout the book when explaining different situations. Feel free to insert yourself or anyone you know when reading about stuff that relates to your life.

Please Don't Sue Us

In this book, we deal with some pretty heavy issues, some of which we have personal experience with and some we don't. We researched the heck out of the stuff and tried our best to give you the facts in the most clear-cut way. But we're writers, not doctors. If you feel like you need more than this book offers, by all means, seek it out.

Acknowledgments

Thanks to our great families, terrific boyfriends, and super-duper best friends. You're the glue that keeps us together, in line, and relaxed enough to be able to write a book about stress management. Thanks to Andree Abecassis, the coolest agent around, and Randy Ladenheim-Gil at Alpha for having the confidence in us to handle this project.

Special Thanks to the Technical Reviewer

The Complete Idiot's Guide to Dealing with Stress for Teens was reviewed by an expert who double-checked the accuracy of what you'll learn here, to help us ensure that this book gives you everything you need to know about teens and stress. Special thanks are extended to Donna M. Simmons, a Research Associate at the University of Southern California who is completing a Neuroscience Ph.D. on a part of the brain that controls stress. A biographee of *Who's Who of American Women* with interests in communication, behavior, and stress, Donna has lectured on "The Biological Basis of the Stress Response" and conducted workshops for medical laboratory professionals on "Managing Stress in your Life and your Lab." Originally from the Seattle area, Donna is an outdoor enthusiast and mountain climber who now lives in Los Angeles where she hikes local mountain trails with husband Cory and fellow Neuroscience graduate students.

Trademarks

All terms mentioned in this book that are known to be or are suspected of being trademarks or service marks have been appropriately capitalized. Alpha Books and Pearson Education, Inc. cannot attest to the accuracy of this information. Use of a term in this book should not be regarded as affecting the validity of any trademark or service mark. .

The Stress Mess

Stress has been a part of your life since day one. When you were little, so were your problems. But now as you head into your teen years, the pressure is mounting and you're not sure why. All of a sudden, just getting through the day feels like a struggle. You're suddenly faced with more choices and opportunities than ever before. Instead of feeling lucky, you feel overwhelmed, and it's hard to know what to do about it.

In the first four chapters of this book, we'll explain what stress is exactly, where it comes from, and how it affects your life. We'll pinpoint exact sources and explain how it can make you feel, both physically and emotionally. So pick a spot to get comfy, grab some munchies, and get ready to brush up on the basics of stress.

Chapter 1

The World Can Be Heavy, Give Your Shoulders a Rest

In This Chapter

- Under pressure
- What's your cause?
- Sensitive to the strain
- You're in good company

Your parents are on your back, your friends need you, you have a term paper due in a week, and you can't tell if that cutie from bio was flirting with you or just had a twitchy eye. You are undeniably, certifiably stressed out. And you just know that as soon as this wave of chaos is over, you'll be swimming as fast as you can to avoid the next one. Stress is a fact of life for everyone, and it's been around forever, so you don't have to feel stressed about feeling stressed. In this chapter, we'll take a look at the stress thing, where it comes from, and how learning to dodge it early will save you lots of trouble in the future.

This Thing Called Stress

When did life get so complicated? These days, it seems like you've got lots of problems and issues and stuff that's just bugging the heck out of you. And it's a constant thing. You feel pulled in a million directions by a jillion different people, when all you really want to do is sit still for a minute. You're stressed out, and you need shelter from this crazy tornado of a lifestyle.

Well, you'll be happy to know that you're not the first privileged teen to be awarded the tarnished trophy of stress. It's a feeling as old as time, actually as old as mankind, and it's completely normal. Stress is what you feel when faced with a problem of any kind, big or small. Deciding which sweatshirt to wear to school causes stress. Your computer screen freezes, and you're stressed. Mom catches you breaking curfew ... again. Guess what you're feeling? Yup, you got it. Stress.

Let's picture the world back in the day when cavewomen and cavemen roamed the land. Things were much different back then. The women wore bones in their hair instead of butterfly clips, and the men sat around after dinner scratching themselves and grunting. Okay, so maybe not much has changed.

Life was pretty rough back then for ol' CaveMarty and CaveMarcy. Food was scarce, life was uncertain, and danger was everywhere. Forget gigabytes and DVDs—this was a time when rubbing two sticks together to make a fire was high-tech. Plus, everyone was just trying to get used to walking upright.

Anyway, when confronted with something new and unexpected that was potentially dangerous, the body reacted in a way that was meant to protect itself. This is called the "fight or flight" reaction. Let's say CaveMarty and his buds went out to hustle some grub for CaveMarcy, the sistahs, and the cavekids. They weren't in the mood for burritos, so the guys went hunting for wooly beasties instead. Well, the boys were in for quite a surprise when the beastie they were after turned on them and charged. Holy Ice Age, CaveMarty, you'd better take action! And quick!

Thanks to the miracle of biology, chemicals were released in their bodies to help get them ready to protect themselves. They had two choices of how to react to the situation: fight the beastie or run for the hills. The beastie was pretty huge, so the guys took off as fast as their cavelegs could carry them and looked elsewhere for a more co-operative dinner. Thank goodness for their bodies' response to the stress. They could have ended up as the beastie's dinner instead.

Today our bodies are pretty much the same as Marty's and Marcy's were back then. Well, except that we're probably a bit sweeter-smelling and better moisturized. But we are living inside our own caveman bodies in the modern world. Most of us don't hunt for our dinners, but we still feel stresses of our own that are just as strong, and our bodies react to them today the same way they always have.

Besides the causes of our stress, other factors in the equation have also changed. The way we react to stress is totally different now. In most modern social situations, running and fighting are not good responses. Imagine if your algebra teacher started handing out a pop quiz and, in a state of panic, you run out the door like you're trying out for the Olympics. Probably an inappropriate response. But you still get this feeling like you want to fight or flee. What do you do? You have to find other ways to deal with your stress.

Where the Beast Is Born

Stress comes from a variety of situations. We all know them, and we all experience them. Ever been faced with a decision that leaves you totally clueless about how to handle it? Yeah, so do we. Big deci-sions, little decisions—they can all feel like abominable tasks. Whether you have 2 things to choose from or 50, you could debate for hours trying to pick the right one. These days, you're faced with more choices than ever: a grocery store aisle full of cereals, 500 cable channels, hundreds of colleges, thousands of possible careers. Aaaah! Sometimes it feels like too much—how could you possibly pick the right one?

Then there's the stress of success. We all know that one well. You want to be good at the stuff you do, even the stuff you're not that into. It would be great to be great all the time. Smartest in your class, coolest in your grade, best looking on the team—you need to succeed in lots of areas to feel happy, at least, that's what it seems like. If you do well at school, you get into a good college and then start an amazing, fun, and fulfilling career. And it sometimes feels like every test you take and every grade you get can get you closer to that. Heavy.

Beware of Burnout

You have emotional needs that you're desperate to have filled. You want to be accepted by the people you like, and you also wouldn't mind a little romance, even though it sometimes feels like that'll never happen. You get stressed thinking about how, if, or when you'll get these things. Try not to let it get to you. With confidence and patience, you'll always find ways to fulfill them.

The desire to succeed is really strong, and so is the fear of failure. If you don't really try at something and then fail at it, you're not surprised. You're not happy, but you're not surprised. Then there are times when you do really try: You study for the test or you practice so that you'll make the team. Sometimes you fail then, too. How frustrating! Trying and failing at piano lessons, or at an interview for an after-school job can make you feel like a giant zero.

Then there's that stress that you would never think would be a problem until you experience it. Sometimes having too much freedom can be stressful. This might make you laugh, but it's absolutely true. Things get so crazy; you're unsure about so much, and you have mixed feelings about everything else. You need someone or something to give you some guidance. Rules can be annoying, but at least you know where you stand. You can choose to follow them or break them, but, the truth is, there's still structure there.

Keepin' It Real

"When my mom got her new job, she had long hours and was barely around. We couldn't have dinner at six every night like we used to. Sometimes she was so tired when she got home, we just ordered pizza and ate it in front of the TV. It used to be fun when we did that once in a while. It's not fun any more."

—Ally, age 13

Okay, so too much freedom freaks you out, but so does too little. Free time is also a necessary part of your schedule that helps you stay balanced. The super-villain always out to destroy your free time is Over-Commitment. Your schedule is jam-packed, and there never seems to be a break in sight. Who knows when you'll get a second to breathe. How annoying is that? The stuff you're busying yourself with had better be worth it because it's taking time away from that hobby of all hobbies: chilling out.

Life is a series of constant ups and downs that are uncontrollable and unpredictable. Big life changes and milestones, whether positive or negative, can really throw you for a loop. People are creatures of habit, and change can be completely off-putting, making you wobbly and feeling lost. Graduation is a major moment in life. If your family decides to move, your world can turn upside down. The death of a loved one, or anyone you know, is probably the biggest curveball of all. These events are never easy to get through, but you can prevail and end up even stronger in the end.

Some stresses are constant, like a fly buzzing in your ear. You may be so used to them, you don't even notice them anymore. Live in a noisy neighborhood? That's a constant stress. Parents always fighting? Stress. Is the radio or TV always on in your house? These things are stressing you out, and you might not even know.

Stress puts a strain on your relationships, affects your mood, and can even make you sick. There are lots of ways you can deal with these things. Too bad some of the really obvious ways don't work. You can bury your head in the sand in an attempt to hide from the stuff that's bothering you. Some teens try to avoid their problems by ignoring them or sleeping through them. Maybe you've even faked being sick just so you could stay home and miss the test you didn't study for. Some students go so far as to cut the class. Well, surprise, surprise. When you go back to school, the test is still there. You can distract yourself by doing anything under the sun rather than dealing with the real issue.

Procrastination is a seductive but dangerous thing. People can be really creative, coming up with activities just to put off the inevitable. Some will do anything they can to get away from the stuff that stresses them out. The dumb, destructive, and wrong thing to do is hit the bottle or use drugs. Of course, we all know these things are bad news and offer only a temporary escape. Your real problems are still unsolved.

There are good, healthy ways to slay the stress beast. You and you alone are in control of how you think and deal with stress. You can put a stop to the madness. Read on, and we'll show you how.

Touchy Feely

During the teen years, you're exposed to lots of new outside forces that are responsible for a lot of the chaos in your life. You are also probably increasingly aware of what's going on inside. That stuff, the stuff in your heart and in your head, piles more real pressures onto your already substantial stack.

It's important for everyone to feel included and be part of the group. This desire becomes megastrong at this time in your life. Friends are a huge part of your day-to-day life; sometimes they probably feel even more essential to you than your family. Beyond just having good friends, you want to feel a part of something. That's where the group thing comes in. Everyone wants to feel accepted. Other people liking you reassures you that you're a-okay, you're cool, and you're definitely doing something right, even if you're not sure what it is.

Keepin' It Real

"I act like I don't care what anybody thinks about me. But if I ever hear that someone at school says something nasty about me, I totally lose sleep. I can't help it. I know it shouldn't matter, but it does."

—Carrie, age 15

The big worry behind not having a group to call your own—or, worse yet, being excluded from one—is being different from the norm. Yeah, yeah, people talk about diversity and uniqueness, but that's all easier to swallow if you can also fit in. The ironic thing about all this is the uncertainty about what is or what *should* be considered normal.

Come on! In a world with this many choices and with this many types, attitudes, and personalities of people, how could you possibly determine what's normal? It's also interesting to consider the fact that the really cool people in the world, and probably those in your school, must be different than everyone else in some way. But, chances are, being different is okay if you're different in what you think is the "right" way.

Teens worry about being different behaviorally as well. You may wonder if you walk weird, talk weird, or think weird. When you go shopping, you probably go out of your way to make sure you buy the same brand or look of clothes that your buds at school wear. Don't feel guilty about it. Fitting in is fine. It gives you a sense of belonging and normalcy, and it can be comforting. But it's always the people who go out on a limb or take a chance that really get noticed. It's not a bad thing to stand out from the crowd, and it's especially great to stand at the head of it.

Doing your own thing is a risky business. You can never really be sure how it's going to turn out. Will you come out of it a leader, or the kid no one wants to sit with at lunch? No one can predict that, and not knowing is a scary thing. With things changing so fast in your teens, it's hard to know where any path will lead you. You feel like you're walking through some unfamiliar, enchanted forest with a blindfold on, just hoping you'll get out unscathed. Your body and your soul are headed into the unknown, and you're not sure how to handle it.

And what if you haven't gone through all of these changes yet? Who knows what these changes are going to be like, anyway? Looking at the pictures in your health book and giggling in class when the teacher says *those words* is one thing, but who knows what it will be like for you?

If the future of your own bod is uncertain, the future of everything else is even more up in the air. Picking classes is hard when you don't know what you're in for—same with picking a sweetheart, a college, or a career. The way to conquer this stress? Just go for it. Try making one small decision; you don't have to figure the whole thing out at once. But just hold your nose and do your best cannon-ball right into that mysterious pool of doubt and uncertainty.

Imagine for a second that one of the seniors in your Spanish class invites you to a blowout party this weekend. You're not sure how to feel about this. Is it a blessing or a curse? You can't even tell. On one hand, it will probably be a killer party. All the coolest kids will be there, maybe even your crush-of-the-week. On the other hand, it's bound to be mostly older kids, and you're only a freshman. You can't believe you even got invited. But what if no one talks to you? What if your clothes aren't right? What if you end up being the dork alone in the corner while everyone else whispers rude things about you? It's too much to think about! Better skip it!

Okay, slow down for a minute. You're letting your imagination run away with you, and it's stressing you out. When you don't know what to expect, it's very easy to get scared off. It's that fear of the unknown that's making you worry like crazy about all kinds of random hypothetical scenarios. The truth is, you can't possibly know what the party will be like. No one can. But once you jump into something new, you've done it. It'll never be scary again because you've already been there, done that. If you avoid things just because they're unfamiliar, you'll stay inexperienced and scared. The party could end up being a wild time and could totally make your whole high school experience. But if you let yourself get all tied up in the "what ifs", you may end up missing out.

Keepin' It Real

"I really wanted to play football at my new school. But when I got there, everyone else had already tried out. I would have to do it alone. I ended up blowing it off. These guys looked a lot bigger than the guys at my last school anyway. It sucks, 'cause I totally miss playing."

—Chris, age 16

At times you can't control the situations you walk into, but by taking the initiative, you can make these times less scary. Learn as much as you can about what you're getting into ahead of time. That way The Great Unknown won't be nearly that mysterious. Ask around to find out who else is going to the party, what time they're getting there, and maybe even what they're wearing. And drag one of your pals along with you. They'd probably be thrilled to get the invite, and you'll have a built-in support system, someone to hang with all night, just in case the party is less than stellar. You'll be fine. You're a cool cat yourself, and they should be happy you'd go to their party, anyway.

All of these stresses can make you feel like a walking raw nerve. (Eww, what an image.) They can sometimes wind you so tight that your head feels like it's about to explode, and your attitude isn't much better. Your moods are strongly affected by stress, and your feelings are often heightened. You're more sensitive than usual—just ask the people around you. Your mom tells you that your shirt's wrinkled, and you jump down her throat, yell some stuff you shouldn't, and then storm out of the room. That poor woman! She's talking laundry, and you're taking it personally. But you can't help it, either. You're just on edge. You're full of anxiety over lots of little things, but you just couldn't care less about other stuff. You're also becoming quite a cynic in your old age, and defensive, too.

Stress upsets everyone, so don't let these feelings and responses surprise you. Many people have unrealistic expectations of the world and are surprised when things don't work out. Of course, life can rock, but not always. We all know that things don't always happen the way we want or expect them to. You've got to get real and accept that. The world is full of positive, good things, and life can be a blast, but you have to accept the bad with the good. Take time to be especially happy and thankful when things go well, and try to be calm when they don't.

That sounds like a heck of a plan, but we know it's easier said than done. You can try to control your feelings, but often they can get away from you and head right down the Highway of Confusion. The best thing you can do to combat this is to keep tabs on your feelings. When life gets hectic, it's easy to push your emotions aside—after all, who needs more clouds when you already feel foggy? But resist that urge and get in touch with your inner self. Acknowledging how you feel—whether happy, upset, in love, frustrated, whatever—helps you breathe a little easier.

A great way to let your emotions hang loose is the old-fashioned method—cry them out. Crying is a physical response to certain stresses. It releases the super-charger adrenaline, which is why you feel refreshed after a good bawling session. And for those of you tough guys and tough gals out there who think crying is for wimps, get a clue! If you don't want people to see you turn on the water works, fine. Just go somewhere quiet and alone, and let it all out.

Stress is exhausting. It can wear you down if you don't take the time to refuel. You lose your edge. You get sloppy and feel tired, like you got in a fight with a wrecking ball and lost. Eventually you just get burned out, which is a sorry state to be in. You start losing your true inner connections to stuff you used to be into. Soon you're just going through the motions. But it doesn't have to go that far! You can handle your life, your body, your emotions, and the way you deal with them. Be the captain of your own ship. You can steer it to calmer, cooler waters when you learn to exercise your stress control!

Everyone Feels the Crunch

Stress is natural and effects everyone. George Washington felt total stress. Think about it: The guy had a lot on his plate. So did Honest Abe and Martin Luther King Jr. They had the majorest of major issues to worry about.

And you don't have to be a big-shot political figure or civil rights leader to feel the burn. Think about your favorite sports stars and movie stars. They have so many people waiting on them and expecting things from them that they must be totally freaked out sometimes. What if they forget a line? Or miss a basket? We're talking big money and careers at stake, let alone the huge embarrassment factor if you mess up. And how about all the rock stars and boy-band boys? Imagine going up in front of a huge crowd every night just to have people staring at you! Those rocker boys must get totally stressed. Probably more than you do worrying about your English paper, so don't feel too sorry for yourself if you have to stay in this weekend to finish it. No matter how frantic you feel, there's someone out there who's got it even crazier.

Fighting the Funk

Stress can be a positive force. It can push you or inspire you to try something that you ordinarily wouldn't have. It may even influence you to try harder to excel at something. Learn to combat the bad stress, and let the good shine through!

Everyone, including your friends, your parents, cowboys, and astronauts, feels the squeeze and deals with the same issues in life. That means they're prone to the same mood swings and the same short temper you are. We all experience rejection, failure, drama, crisis, and death. So when you see someone stressed out, do that person a favor and cut him some slack. If you know that your pal's going through a nutty period, try to understand. Put yourself in his cross-trainers for a second and be patient. And if someone isn't getting you, explain your situation. That person will dig it because you've all been in that boat before and you all know how un-fun it can be.

Everyone deals with stress differently. You probably learned a lot about attitude from your family and the way you were raised. How do your parents handle situations? Are they calm? Excitable? Laid back? That's probably what you do, too. Is that way working for you? If you're reading this book, chances are good that it's not. You can change the way you look at things and the way you cope. Stick with us, and we'll explain how. If you learn to deal with it now and get a good method down, you'll be able to handle it better in the future. Sorry to say, stress doesn't go away when you hit 20.

The Least You Need to Know

- Stress is a completely normal feeling caused by countless factors, such as too many freedoms, too many choices, and over-committing yourself.

- Bad methods of coping, like denial or substance abuse, will only avoid or mask the true problem at hand.

- Stress wreaks havoc physically, mentally, and emotionally, even though many worries and expectations are often all in your head.

- Everyone experiences stress. Try to be understanding of others, since everyone deals differently.

Chapter 2

Growing Up Is Hard to Do

In This Chapter

- All grown up
- Careening toward adulthood
- Generation gap
- Grace under fire

So you've made it off the playground, out of junior high, and into the thick of young adulthood. Life begins now! Or so you thought. Along with lots of new responsibilities, social pressures, and an expanded intellect come tougher decisions, greater consequences, and added academic demands. It's exciting to think that the world is your oyster, but it is also overwhelming. Hang in there, and you will definitely make it through. The one thing you can count on is that everyone else is just as confused as you are; they're just not talking about it, either.

Everyone goes through an awkward stage, is torn by insecurities, and occasionally makes a fashion *faux pas*. Each day it seems like there are a million things that could go wrong, and some days they will. But with a little preparation, you'll be able to move through the next few years in this new, exciting, but scary world of possibilities with a little more confidence and attitude than the next teen.

Welcome to the Teen Age

Whether you realize it or not, stress has always been a part of your life. Think back to kindergarten and getting tackled by the girl who ate paste. Wow! Who would have thought she would be so ticked off about losing a game of hopscotch? Then you went on to first grade and a whole new series of stresses: Your first spelling test. Your first part in a school play (that Chicken Little costume was not your idea). And what about class trips? Those alone could cause massive amounts of anxiety: remembering to have your permission slip signed, packing an extra-big lunch, making sure you sat next to your friend on the bus, trying not to get lost at the museum/library/historical monument, picking out a souvenir, and, finally, making it home in one piece. Whew! In those days, that was quite a challenge.

Nowadays the stakes are way higher. You're trying to deal with the simultaneous development of your mind and your body—and look cool while doing it! As you get older, both start to change and become more complicated. Sometimes it even seems like your body has a mind of its own. Depending on your age and your genes, you may be taller, shorter, fatter, or thinner than everyone else in your class. And the comparisons don't stop there. Smarter, dumber, prettier, uglier, richer, poorer—but never just right. Teenagers tend to focus on the superficial, so if that stunning personality of yours is hiding under a big nose or untamable hair, you might feel lower than low. Chances are, you aren't happy with what fate and your parents have blessed you with in the body department.

Physical development is stressful because it never happens to two people the same way, making everyone feel like a freak. Your body is maturing, and your emotions are not far behind. Understand that, at this time in your life, everything is majorly intensified. Emotional highs and lows will make you feel like you're riding on your very own hormone roller coaster. Stuff that never bothered you before will suddenly become earth-shattering. Picture it: You're finally hanging with the cool kids at lunch, and you realize that you have the better half of that jumbo chocolate chip cookie you just scarfed down stuck in your braces. Two years ago you would have thought that was hilarious and pointed it out to everyone. Not anymore.

Keepin' It Real

"In junior high, I was the class clown, always kidding around with everyone. But like a month ago, my voice started getting weird, like cracking and stuff. It's embarrassing, and now I don't talk in class so much anymore."

—Kevin, age 13

The last thing you want to do is talk about these confusing and very personal changes with anyone you feel might not understand or, worse yet, might betray your confidence. Deciding who to talk to about serious stuff and all these firsts in your life is not easy. Your parents, who at one time were a great source of comfort, may now seem too out of touch and infinitely uncool. A hug from Mom or a chat with Dad is no longer enough to ease the pain. They just don't get it. Your dad complains that paying bills and sitting in traffic is stressful for him, and he's right—but what you're dealing with is not the same. This is not your parents' stress. You have your own special brand of teen issues. How could they possibly remember their first kiss or the first time they majorly flunked an important exam?

The next few years are especially crucial because you're figuring out *who you are*. You're probably thinking, "I know who I am. My name's Alex, I'm 14 years old, I live in Scranton, and I hate my little brother." That's not what we mean. We mean, what are your likes and dislikes? Are you into Top 40 music or underground punk? Do you have any idea of what kind of career you'd like when you get older? Are you an artist, an activist, an atheist? You may be all these things, or you may be none of them. You don't have to decide now. The point is, a bunch of new ideas and concepts are being thrown at you now. With no direction or guidance, the stuff feels like it's just bouncing around your brain with nowhere to land. The world is full of information and choices; you want to be, and choose, the things that you feel best represent you as an individual.

As you're absorbing all these new ideas and issues, you're bound to come across some that are troubling. There's the more basic unpleasant stuff, like when you see someone totally innocent accused of cheating on an exam at school. Then there are the bigger, heavier issues, like learning about children in foreign countries dying of starvation, the depletion of the ozone layer, or the threat of nuclear war. Yikes! Crawling back into your bunk bed is one option, but sooner or later, you have to come out.

Keepin' It Real

"I used to read the paper with my dad in the mornings, but I stopped because it made me sad. Every day, it seemed like only bad things were happening in the world, and then I would think about them for the rest of the day. It was too depressing."

—Kelly, age 14

Along with being introduced to an adult world comes learning to deal with some of the tragedy and injustice within it. This can be very distressing and sometimes may make you feel like you're not ready to handle such major stuff. Especially when so much of it seems to go against the values and ideals that your parents taught you—to share your toys, always say please and thank you, and not beat up your little sister. It all seemed so simple then. What we learn as teens is that the world is a very big and complicated place. There are different kinds of governments, cultures, and languages.

Wars break out and people die. Maybe even your relatives or some-one you know dies. Does that make the world evil? No, but it isn't always fair, either.

Things happen to us every day that are out of our control, and that can be really frustrating. Feeling helpless is a big part of feeling stressed, particularly when part of you is so anxious to prove your-self to those around you. At times like this, you can really feel pulled in two directions. You want to be an individual, but you also want to fit in.

While you're forming these great opinions about the world and de-veloping your own theories about the complexities of life, you're also probably hoping that your ideas are not too different from your friends'. But at the same time that we are growing and becoming in-dependent thinkers, we also desperately want to have opinions that other kids share. It takes some practice, but eventually you will learn to mesh popular opinion with your own individuality. Remember, there is a natural pace to life, and your teen years are a part of that. Some change needs to happen gradually so that you can prepare for it. Hang in there, try to be patient, and don't obsess about what you can't control.

Twenty-First Century Syndrome

As if all the inner changes you're going through aren't stressful enough, teens face an especially tough time dealing with the outside difficulties of our modern society. We live in a fast-paced, high-pressure world, and no one knows that better than you. Maybe both your parents work and you feel like you never see them. Is dinner-time always rushed so that everyone can finish activities or home-work before bed? Do you sometimes bolt out of bed in the morning automatically assuming that you are late for something? Do each of your family members angle for private computer time at home? And that's when you're not in school, studying for the SATs, or practic-ing parallel parking.

There is so much to do, so much to know, and so much to have. Where do you begin, and how do you keep up? There is no definite answer, but managing your life, your schedule, and your stress is a great start.

Beware of Burnout

Kids today face overwhelming problems, hectic schedules, and very grown-up situations. Don't feel pressured to handle it all on your own. Ask for help when you need it.

Life in the Fast Lane

In high school, much of your time is spent preparing for college, and that means thinking about a major course of study. The idea of being a doctor or lawyer is almost old-fashioned. These days jobs like web designers, graphic artists, aerospace engineers, and veejays are hot careers available to you. Where do you even begin?

Today's teens don't want to just make a lot of dough; they want to be happy while they do it. Having it all today means holding down a great job, raising a family, and having the money to do the things you like in your spare time. People are tired of being slaves to their jobs. They want to be fulfilled, and have fun, too.

As a teenager, you have lots of time to prepare for your future, and you have the benefit of being part of the most plugged-in group of people in the world. Teens are up on all the cool trends before everyone else is, so use this time in your life to check out what's out there. Read the newspaper, watch TV, and ask questions. Find out what careers interest you and what job skills suit your special abilities. Sometimes what we're good at naturally can become the way we earn our living as adults. You'll be most successful and happy in life when you're doing something you truly enjoy.

In exploring new ideas and keeping an eye on what others are doing, try to keep in mind that not everybody who seems to have a perfect life actually does. Inevitably, you'll come across people whose lives seem absolutely peachy. You imagine that if you could just switch places with them, your life would be, too. Not true. Lots of our examples of grown-up living come from television and the movies, and celebrities are not necessarily the best examples of reality. Physically, most actors and actresses are gorgeous creatures who look like they've never battled acne or calculus. Don't be fooled by their current appearances or seemingly great lives. There is hard work, determination, and sometimes many years of practice behind that now glamorous existence. Behind the scenes, no one's life is perfect. So, try not to get caught up in envying what others seem to have. Instead, work on perfecting what you've already got.

Fighting the Funk

Don't get caught up in keeping up. Obsessing over what someone else has doesn't work. Pave your own way.

The best part of the millennium age is the range of its diversity. There is now a bigger window of what's acceptable in career, hobbies, friends, and family structure, making it easier for people to be true to themselves.

Growing Up Gracefully

Dealing with your future will require maturity, patience, self-control, and confidence. Sound impossible? It's not. You may feel like you don't have any of these traits right now, but you will. It will just take some practice.

Another essential element of balancing your life and managing your stress is cultivating healthy self-esteem. That means believing in yourself and the choices you make. Believing that you are good, smart, and worthy will be the most important quality to have in the coming years. It will give you the confidence to make tough decisions and accept that when things don't go your way, it's not necessarily because you screwed up. Things happen for a number of reasons, and we all make mistakes; we just need to make sure we learn from them. Surviving in a fast-paced world requires stress-busting tools to make your everyday challenges easier to deal with.

Sometimes a series of stressful things happen in a row, making their total effect much worse than if each thing had happened individually. Imagine that you wake up late on a Monday morning. Already rushed, you can't find the shirt you planned to wear. You waste time that you don't have looking for it and still come up empty-handed. Rummaging through your hamper, all you can find to match the jeans you've already put on is your least favorite sweater. Ugh. When you get to school, your locker jams, you trip in front of the hottie transfer student in class, and you realize that you forgot your homework for first period. By lunchtime you are ready to snap.

Sound familiar? These kinds of crazy days happen often when we're under pressure. The events of the day snowball, and finally we explode at something little that wouldn't normally bother us. Since we can't always avoid these kinds of days, at least we can recognize that we are on edge and a little sensitive. Warn your friends, if you have to. They'll thank you for it later.

Keepin' It Real

"One day last semester seriously seemed like the worst day of my life. First thing in the morning I found out that I didn't get the lead in the school play. Then I got sick from my burger at lunch. I was in such a bad mood for the rest of the afternoon, I completely screwed up my driver's test and flunked!"

—Samantha, age 17

One of the worst things you can do is play the victim. Bad days happen to all of us. Exaggerating your situation or playing it up for sympathy will probably only annoy those around you. Don't blame anyone else for what's going on with you. Be straightforward about the situation. Everyone will appreciate your honesty and probably will be more likely to cut you some slack. Handling problems this way also gives you back some of the control you feel you've lost being at the mercy of snowballing setbacks.

Choosing the way you're going to handle a situation automatically gives you some power over it. And remember, at the end of a really bad day, when you're lying in bed with the covers over your head crying, "Why me?", remember that there's always tomorrow and a chance for things to go more smoothly. If you're really in over your head, admit it. Don't procrastinate. Talk to someone relevant and explain the situation. Asking for help is sometimes embarrassing, but getting the assistance you need during crunch times can be a huge relief.

Also try to keep yourself balanced, and avoid obsessing over one aspect of your life. With school, your social life, and extracurricular activities soaking up so much of your time, you might feel spread a little thin, but it can be good for you in the long run. Being involved in a variety of things and hanging out with different groups of people makes you a "renaissance" teen, someone who can't be stereotyped or left behind. Becoming too focused on a budding romance or reliving your flubbed oral report over and over again in your mind will not be helpful in any way. Dwelling on stuff too much only confuses you more and distorts the situation. The more you think about something after the fact, the more you lose perspective on what actually happened.

At the end of the day, everyone can think of things they wished they'd done differently or times they could have acted more suavely. Part of growing up is being able to admit we aren't perfect. There are daily obstacles and challenges facing all of us, but with a basic understanding of stress and how it affects us, we can get through the good times as well as the rough patches. Healthy, happy people are able to laugh at themselves and some of the sticky situations that pop up along the way.

The Least You Need To Know

- Stress has always been a part of your life, but once you become a teenager, it seems to double by the hour.

- Physical and mental changes are happening so quickly that it sometimes feels impossible to get through a day. Hang in there, and you'll make it through the storm.

- Being a teenager these days means dealing with a whole slew of experiences unique to your generation.

- Armed with a little patience and some stress-busting tools, you can minimize the growing pains of your teen years.

Chapter 3

The Inside Jive

In This Chapter

- Can you cut it?
- Shushing the voices in your head
- Apples and sushi
- The laws of flaws

Stress is coming at you from all angles, and it's happening constantly. You are forced to find ways to deal with it just to preserve your own sanity. Lately it's been a full-time job, and you're exhausted. If only you could stop these stresses at the source. But wait! You do have the power to control one thing: yourself. The pressures you put on yourself can be excessively and unnecessarily strong. In this chapter, we'll examine the ways people stress themselves out and get a jump on how to get yourself off the hook.

Your Own Worst Enemy

Sure, the world is a tough place to live, full of forces beyond your control. Everything is constantly in motion, and you are at the mercy of all this, smack dab in the middle of the action and riddled with factors that stress you out. But many people, especially teens, compound their problems by working themselves into a frenzy over them.

During the hectic teenage years, the world seems to be spinning around you. Your body's popping and buzzing, your thoughts are rockin' and rollin', and you feel like you're finally growing up. It sometimes feels like you're riding down a dirt road in a car with three flat tires. Ouch! You're sensitive and confused, and, frankly, you're not always thinking straight or seeing clearly. On top of that you have your dramatic moments (you know who you are!).

We've all obsessed over something at one time or another: a crush, an exam, an audition. Maybe you were desperate to make a team or to buy a specific pair of way-overpriced sneakers. Or maybe you've driven yourself nuts reliving an incident, like a conversation you had with that cutie after school. Did she like you? Did you make a fool of yourself? Did she even care? You feel like you could crack the code if you thought about it enough. Sometimes we just can't get things out of our heads. You get caught in a loop of thinking that you can't seem to break out of. Get your mind off your obsession by switching gears. The best way to keep your mind off one thing is to focus on something else.

Fighting the Funk

The time you spend worrying is all wasted. It's natural to be concerned about certain things, especially things that really affect you. But teens often exceed their normal worry duties and get a little silly about the small, unimportant things that they spend their time obsessing over.

Dwelling on them makes things into a way bigger deal in your mind than it ever was in reality. Getting hooked on an idea or hung up on a concept makes it snowball into a monstrosity of focus. And your imagination kicks into overdrive, creating all kinds of crazy scenarios. You fixate on and get upset over a magnified version of what's really going on, turning a small incident or problem into a huge one. Sure, the situation may have been a little stressful, but in actuality, you are responsible for having succeeded in stressing yourself out.

One of the traps teens fall into is worrying about things they can't change or have no control over. It's like sitting around all upset about your favorite band breaking up or that it's raining on your birthday. Why bother? Things like this will happen constantly, and while they may be upsetting, they're beyond you. Ask yourself, "What is the worst that could happen?" Chances are, the worst-case scenario is not nearly as horrible as you imagine. If you have a real emotional stake in the matter, you're perfectly entitled to "take a moment." But after that, move up and on, and instead pay attention to the things you can control, affect, or make go the way you want.

Keepin' It Real

"My boyfriend was being real weird and quiet for like three straight days, and it made me so upset. I was sure that was it. I thought he probably liked someone else. We finally talked like the next day, and it turned out he was just nervous about a project he was doing for class. I got all scared over nothing."

–Julie, age 15

The same worry rules apply to hypothetical situations. That's when you imagine a scenario that might happen and ask yourself "what if?" "What if I get the lowest SAT score ever recorded and can't get into a good college?" "What if when I ask Betty Sue to the dance, she pats me on the head and then points at my cowlick and laughs with her friends? I'll never be able to show my face in this school again." Okay, hang on. Here we go with that overactive imagination again. First of all, you're probably not a psychic with your own late-night infomercial, so how could you even pretend to be able to predict the future? Making an educated guess is one thing, but jumping ahead and getting yourself all worked up over something that probably won't happen causes total self-imposed stress.

Sometimes you can actually leave yourself open to an imagined destruction, allowing it to come true. A "self-fulfilling prophecy" is when you think something bad will happen, so you don't do anything to prevent it. Then when it happens, you think, "See, I knew it." Like if you're sure you won't get into choir because you just know you'll screw up the tryouts, you've already given up in your head. So what happens at tryouts? You hit those high notes worse than a cat in heat, and you don't get in. You think, "See, I knew it!" But if you concentrated and sang like that old soul singer who you know lives inside you, you would have gotten in, no problem. You actually sabotaged yourself.

When you focus on something, you move toward it, like a moth to a flame, even if it's what you don't want to happen. This is a natural function of concentration, of focus, that can be a trap if you obsess about things. Think about when you first started driving and were sure you'd go in the ditch or cross over the center line by just trying to stay away from it.

Worrying your little head off over silly things does not help and will only make you more frustrated. It's counterproductive. If you're faced with a real problem, solve it. But if it's just a "situation" you can't really control, don't mull it over and make yourself crazy.

And remember, just because you're thinking or feeling something doesn't mean that it's true or that it ever will be a fact. The only thing you can really control in this mad, crazy world is yourself. Don't get all wound up in stuff you can't control, like what people say or think about you. An overall positive attitude is important to have. Be an optimist—you know, one of those glass-half-full people. There's no reason to always assume the worst. Things rarely get anywhere near that bad.

Insecurity City

Part of the reason why teens tend to assume that dark rain clouds are following them is because they're constantly unsure about themselves. Everyone wants to be the best, funniest, smartest, supercoolest one at school. But does anyone ever feel that way? You may already have a few people in mind who seem to get to live life as one of the pretty and privileged: Well, sure, there's that buxom blonde bombshell who's captain of the tennis team, and that senior guy with the hot sports car and the hotter girlfriend. In your eyes, these people have got it going on, while you're just trying to get something started without stalling out. How could you possibly measure up? You woke up this morning with a zit, took the bus to school, got cut from the field hockey team, and are waiting to have your first kiss. You imagine these other people to have amazingly perfect lives while you're living in their shadows, wallowing in your zit cream and insecurities.

Ask any of those kids who you think are too-cool-for-school how happy they are with themselves, and you'd probably be surprised at what they'd have to say. The blonde is freaking out over possibly flunking trig ... for the second time. And the dude with the sweet ride is taking protein powder to try to put some muscles on what he thinks is a too-skinny frame. And he's also pretty sure that his girlfriend's cheating on him. Everyone's got issues and problems and stuff they wish they could change about themselves, even the people you think have got it all.

But even if you already suspected, it probably doesn't help much. Your insecurities affect the way you see yourself and the way you perceive the world. Are you pretty enough or man enough, and do you dress right? Are you smart enough or too smart? You're worried about feeling inferior to everyone else, but you also don't want to be too superior. And when the heck are you going to lose this darn baby fat? Basically you just want to fit in, but in the right way, the cool way. Life would be way better if you could just somehow make this happen.

But how do you really know the right way stuff is supposed to happen? By looking around, of course. By scoping the scene at school, especially the cool kids, you can tell what's "normal" in all the areas you're concerned with. You see what people are wearing. And you probably want to go with the look of the president of the class rather than the pocket-protector look that the super-nerd in bio is sporting. But you're constantly nervous about how you measure up. Where do you fit on the coolness scale?

Besides just watching what the other kids are doing, you're probably also feeling pressure from other places, like from teachers or parents. Maybe they are pushing you to perform academically or athletically. All these things force you to constantly evaluate yourself. Even if you thought you were doing fine before, pressures from these sources may totally play on your insecurities, making you second-guess yourself and think twice about whether you are doing alright.

Keepin' It Real

"I don't go out a lot on the weekend. It's not like I don't have friends. We sometimes do stuff, but it's not like I go to tons of parties or anything. I'm not really into it–the ones I went to weren't that fun. But my dad is like always asking me about my plans and why I don't have big things to do all the time. I'm happy with the stuff I do. I don't know why he can't be."

–Ben, age 14

It's really too bad that insecurities play such a powerful role in your life. You don't always want to be scrambling to keep up with the other kids. Who wants to run to the mall every time a new fad or trend hits the streets? It has little to do with you and a lot to do with worrying about what others think.

People just want to be liked for who they are, but all this other darn stuff keeps getting in the way. And it's mostly superficial, not who you really are inside. Your true self and your true identity are what people need to see. And you want them to see it, but as much as you hate all that surface stuff, you probably hide behind it, too. It's frustrating to think you could be so different from the way people perceive you—or even the way they want you to be. That's not the real you; it's just somebody walking through the halls.

As difficult as it is, and as unsure as you probably are of yourself, the best thing you can do is be proud of who you are. No matter what others see, you know what you're like underneath. You're interesting and complicated, quirky and sensitive. Be proud of all that, and let it shine through. Building your confidence isn't easy, and it takes time, but when it is firmly in place, you'll have a better, healthier, and more realistic outlook on the world. You'll know when stuff is not your fault, and you'll recognize when you have the power to make the change.

Competition Junction

Your insecurities can keep your confidence level way down and your defenses way up. You're not sure whether you're as good as your peers or whether you'll ever be. In comparing yourself to others, you may develop a competitive edge, desperate to "beat" them at whatever game you can or, worse, feel jealous when others succeed.

Jealousy and competition are actually both natural response that go back to caveman times. Remember our old friends CaveMarty and CaveMarcy? They were competitive and got jealous, too. Back then, they couldn't be slackers and hang around all weekend renting movies and scarfing pizza. They had to keep up with the Cave-Joneses. When Mr. CaveJones and Marty went hunting and food was scarce, it was every man for himself. All those cavemanners went right out the window. And if the CaveCouple saw that the CaveJoneses had more roast beastie to eat for dinner than they did, CaveMarcy would kick CaveMarty's butt to get the heck out there and scare up some more chow. These are part of the survival techniques, and, as with the normal stress responses, they don't have as much a place in today's society as they did back then. But we still feel them, so we have to learn to deal with them.

Constantly comparing yourself to others is never helpful. Sure, you always have your eyes open, keeping tabs on your pals and the other kids at school in an attempt to check yourself and make sure you're doing okay. A certain level of competition is a natural, healthy thing. But, as with everything, there is such a thing as going over-board.

However, life is not fair, and sometimes there is no way to even the playing field. Often you are left mad and frustrated and asking "why?" "Why can't I understand this math when everyone else in class gets it so easily?" "Why can't my parents afford to buy me a car when I get my license?" "Why won't my boobs grow so that I won't look like a 10-year-old boy?" There are no answers to these questions. The fact of the matter is that everyone is different, comes from different types of families, and has different personalities and hair color and senses of humor. How could you possibly compare yourself to them? Or expect to have the same life they do? You probably wouldn't really want theirs, either. You are like apples and sushi. There is no comparison.

Some schools foster a competitive attitude more than others, virtu-ally pitting students against each other in more ways than just who's going to win the talent show. If a school is competitive academically, chances are good that its students are, too. Who got the highest score on the exam or the highest grade on the paper? And things progress from there, continuing throughout the high school years. When the time comes to start thinking about applying to colleges, students get competitive about SATs. After that, they become fo-cused on applications and where everyone's applying. Then they worry about who got accepted where and how they did in compari-son. It's like a never-ending academic hamster wheel that keeps you running in circles focusing on everyone else instead of numero uno, you.

On the flip side, a competitive attitude is not always suffocating and can actually be helpful. By looking at others, you can tell how you're doing. If others are doing more and doing it better and faster, maybe you do need to take a look at why you're lagging be-hind. Don't always feel like you have to live up to the standards of others, but at the same time, make sure you're not performing way below your potential. Is everyone else in class hustling to make the grade and involved in extra-curriculars, to boot, while you're not because you don't feel like it's really "your thing" and you'd much rather lounge around watching game show reruns on TV?

Keepin' It Real

"I'm in college prep classes in school. They're okay, but the kids are so obsessed with their work and grades. When we have a test, they always want to know how everyone else did. I don't even tell them anymore."

–Jen, age 16

Taking yourself off the competitive track does not give you license to be a slacker. Use your own judgment on where to draw the line. Pay attention to others and how they are living their lives and filling their time. Then stop and decide where you think they are going right and wrong. If you're going to take a hint from them, take it from the right place. Don't do the extra credit just to beat Genius Jeanne's grade on the English assignment. Do it because you want to.

You've probably also noticed that the green-eyed monster, jealousy, rears its ugly head when you see something good happen to others that you wish was happening to you. It's a dark, nasty feeling that can be very strong. It can tear you up inside and frustrate you to the point that you just want to stamp your feet and hold your breath until things start to go your way. In the meantime, you're so busy pouting that you've lost focus on yourself and your own real goals, and you tend to fall even further behind. There you go, sabotaging yourself again.

Try not be a brat if someone has or does something enviable. As painful as it may be, you can try to actually be happy for them. Spread this love, and maybe next time something goes well for you, others will be more ready to congratulate you rather than want to knock you down. And seeing others accomplish things and reach their goals can be good for us. It can be encouraging, reminding us that we can do it, too.

Perfect, Shmerfect

Stress can also squeeze the heck out of you if you're one of those people who puts unrealistic expectations on yourself. Perfectionists have it bad, and they often have it because of the pressure that they put on themselves. It's great to want to work hard and expect great things of yourself, but too much of this good thing can be bad news.

Being a teen in the new millennium is all about having more stuff than ever before: more choices, more products, more information, more electronics, more beauty products. It seems like all this stuff is available in better forms than before, too. Everything's "new and improved." But with all this improvement and excess comes added pressure for us to be more improved: faster, better, smarter.

People are better educated these days, and more go to college than in the past. But going to "a" college isn't necessarily enough. You want to go to a "great" college, maybe even the "best" college. You want to have the best sound system and the best computer. You also want to look great, actually better than great. And this quest for perfection stretches through all aspects of our lives. Maybe you want to be the best at the sport you play, too, and be really involved in activities at school. How can you possibly have it all? It's not easy, that's for sure. Actually, it's pretty impossible.

Open up a magazine, and who do you see wearing the clothes? *Super*models. If you didn't feel like you could measure up before, how could you possibly do it now? But seriously, how realistic are these ideals? It's not often you see people who look like that in the real world. The high-profile pretty people are splashed across the pages of magazines, but they are really only one in a million.

Once in a while, reality sets in and slaps you in the face. You wake up in the morning and head to the mirror to take inventory. Okay, nose? Check. Eyes? A little tired, but check. Forehead? Oh, man! What did you do to deserve this? The forehead's there alright, but it looks like you're growing some kind of science experiment on it. You didn't even know they made zits this big. This is not the face of a supermodel. And forget about the body! There's no sense in even starting to list the differences between you and the girl on the cover of the mag, prancing gleefully on the beach, a bikini-clad, rosy-complexioned, impossibly flawless vision of perfection. And forget about the guys! How can anyone be that cool and chiseled? You know what? They can't.

Why do you put yourself through this? Why are you even trying to hold yourself up to this photo that's totally digitally enhanced to look thinner, tanner, and more perfect? They're probably pretty great-looking in person, but they sure ain't perfect. It's not realistic. What you see in the magazine is a total mirage. It's fake, it's fiction, just like actors and actresses on TV and the scripts they act out. They've got lots of people helping them look, act, and sound that great. Plus, they get to do retakes of their make-believe lives just to create the illusion of perfection. You'd be a totally different person, too, if you had that many people fawning over you like that.

Beware of Burnout

You're going through an intense time of growth right now. They don't use the term "awkward phase" for nothing. It sucks that appearance seems so important just at the time your body is freaking out. Don't let yourself get obsessed with looks. Work on feeling good and healthy, and give the superficial stuff a break.

No one is completely happy with his or her body and the way it develops. Girls grow earlier, so they get too tall too fast, while boys have the opposite problem. They worry about having to bring a couple of phone books to the dance to stand on, just so they can mambo with their statuesque dates. And the pounds never seem to go to the right places. Before you know it, girls are dieting and guys are hitting the gym.

Since your body's still changing, your parts are growing at different rates--and sometimes not all together in harmony. Sometimes a physical feature will grow before everything else can catch up. You may feel like your sizeable sniffer is ruining your life, but don't spend too much time worrying about it. Here's a secret for you: You notice your quirks way more than anyone else does. They're all too busy worrying about their own worst features. And besides, these are probably just temporary issues, but you won't be able to tell until you've stopped growing. So don't even think about getting surgery to correct this stuff (unless, of course, it's medically necessary), at least until you're done growing. Remember, your individual looks make you unique. Who wants to look the same as everyone else? How boring would that be, a world of clones? It's like some bad sci-fi flick.

If there are things about your looks that really do bug you or stress you out, focus on the stuff you can change. Your hair is an easy thing, and so are your clothes. Some over-the-counter skin products can improve your complexion, and a new image is easy to achieve with a little style makeover. Then get to work on a mission to look your best. Everyone has plenty of assets; you just tend to lose sight of them when you're being super-critical of yourself.

Putting pressure on yourself to be "the all-around perfect teen" is a cruel thing to do to yourself. You can't expect yourself to do everything right all the time. It just won't happen. And often you're striving for this unrealistic goal based on what you think is expected of you or what other people think is perfect. All you can do is your best. Isn't that what you were always told when you were little? People won't think less of you if you mess up. No one can be brilliant at everything. Learning and experience is valuable, and sometimes you need to get that experience from failing. See, something good does come out of even the crappiest experiences.

The Least You Need to Know

- Stress itself isn't really good or bad. The important thing is how you react to it.

- Insecurities can have a huge effect on how you see yourself and the world around you. The best remedy is to focus on your strengths rather than your weaknesses.

- It's fine to check out what your peers are doing, but be careful not to be too concerned with others.

- Perfection is an impossible state to achieve, although many people become obsessed with attempting it. Work on being the best person you can be.

Chapter 4

Physically Fit to Be Tied

In This Chapter

- Brains 'n bods
- Nervous nellies
- Catchin' Zs
- What's weighing you down
- Troubling times
- Teen trauma

We've already talked about the fact that your body definitely does some internal jumping jacks when you feel stressed out. But beyond that sinking feeling in your stomach lies a whole sea of physical changes that your bod may experience, ranging from the mild to the intense. In this chapter, we'll take a look at the havoc stress can wreak on your mind and body, and how you can reduce daily stress.

The Mind/Body Affair

Whether you plan it or not, your body responds to stressful situations every day by essentially freaking out on you. Your brain is a very powerful machine that gives the go-ahead on a lot of internal stuff before asking your permission. When you experience any stress at all, your mind send a "trouble ahead" telegram to your body, which then gears up for action. You might not even be in that much trouble, but your body doesn't distinguish major from minor, and it responds the same way to almost all stress. Let's face it, realizing that you left your journal in the gym may be mortifying, but it is not life threatening. Nonetheless, your body may react as though you were being attacked by a band of wild cannibals. The effects of stress can be far-reaching physically. Sweaty palms, dry mouth, stomachaches, and skin break-outs are just the tip of the stress iceberg. You may also experience lethargy, fatigue, tense muscles, digestive problems, increase or loss of appetite, sleep disruption, migraine headaches, and backaches. What a blast.

Stressed-out people tend to get sick more often than relaxed types. That's because a stressed-out person has a weaker immune system than someone who's not as fried. Having a lowered immune system means that lots of your defensive cells have gone on vacation, leaving you wide open for monster germs to invade. You know those nagging colds that seem to appear at the worst possible times and then hang around forever, no matter how much vitamin C you pop? There's a good chance that when you were at your phlegm-iest, you were also going through a stressful period in your life.

Fighting the Funk

Focusing on the positive aspects of your life helps you hold your ground when faced with stress. Having a healthy mind is directly related to having a healthy body.

Your emotional state also affects how you feel physically. Some people always seem perky and disgustingly upbeat, while others can be described as "sensitive" or "overly emotional." The way you look at things counts for a lot in determining your overall health. It's hard for teens to realize at this point in their lives that a negative outlook could be influencing their bodies. Not just right now, but also in the years to come. Your annoyingly cheerful friend probably has a better chance of living a long and healthy life than your bummed-out buddy.

Sound scary? It can be. Getting a grip on minor, daily stresses causes enough trouble, but what about when you go through a particularly rocky period that has you tense and anxious for weeks or even months? When you are under pressure for prolonged periods of time, the stakes are raised and so are your chances for developing more serious illnesses, like asthma, ulcers, and migraine headaches.

Keepin' It Real

"I was really excited that my piano recital was coming up, but then right before it, I got all nervous about the things that could go wrong. The more I thought about it, the more my stomach hurt. It felt like someone squeezing my insides."

—Jana, age 14

Countin' Sheep

Stress can affect your sleep schedule, but at what point should you worry? A couple of sleepless nights here and there do not make you an insomniac. Losing sleep the night before a big date or a week before your favorite cousin comes to visit is totally understandable. Nervous anticipation can find you staring at the ceiling at 4 A.M. But when you're really on edge, your sleeping habits may become way different than normal. If you're having trouble falling and staying asleep on a regular basis, it could be because of stress.

Sometimes it's easy to figure out what's keeping you up, while other times the answer is not so clear. You might bolt upright in bed in the middle of the night, sweating and out of breath for no reason—nightmare city. Scary movies or gruesome stories on the news can cause nightmares. But so can worries about a particular event or situation, when that worry comes through in your dreams. If you pay attention to your dreams, you can discover that you're unconsciously upset about things you didn't even realize. Learning the meaning behind your nightmares makes them much less scary and probably less frequent.

Trying to keep a regular sleep schedule is important in keeping your body balanced and relaxed. Getting a good night's sleep—and we're talking at least eight hours—is a great way to make sure you start the day off right. You'll feel rested, recharged, and way more relaxed. Cut some activities short if you have to, to make more room for snoozing. Chatting on the phone with friends or surfing the Net until the wee hours is not always necessary and should be sacrificed sometimes for the sake of catching your zzz's.

But beware of too much sleep—that can getcha, too. Your body's biological clock is reset each day because of your exposure to sunlight. You may look forward to the weekends when you can sleep in, but hitting the sheets and staying there until the sun goes down can be counterproductive. You may think you're resting up, but really you are throwing your body's clock off. It gets used to your weekday schedule. Changing your sleep schedule too drastically on weekends and vacations can actually end up making you feel even more tired.

Fighting the Funk

Getting too much or too little sleep can throw off your body's internal clock, making you feel run-down instead of rested. Keep yourself on a regular sleep schedule for a balanced and relaxed mind and body.

Finally, if none of this is working, here's a hint: Your room could be stressing you out. Your room is your haven. It's set up exactly the way you want it, and it's your little corner of the world. No one is allowed in, and you can do all your TV watching, web browsing, CD listening, and deep thinking in there. And that might be your problem: You do too many other things on your bed besides sleep. Friends sit on it, and you do homework and watch movies on it. Then when it comes time to sleep, you aren't focused on resting. Find another surface for the other activities of your ultra-fabulous life. Pick up a bean bag chair, or drag a grubby one up from the basement. Use your bed only for what it was meant: sleeping.

To Eat or Not to Eat

Parents may get carried away with trying to hide peas in a casserole, but they aren't totally wrong about how good "rabbit food" like fruits and vegetables can be for you. Diet and nutrition play a big part in how good you feel, but it's not something teens think about too often. Arming yourself with a bod that's in tip-top shape makes it harder for the stress meanies to work your nerves.

When stress mounts, it's natural to change your eating habits a little bit. Polishing off a bag of potato chips during a major study session is not unusual, and neither is skipping breakfast the morning of your test because you're too nervous to eat. Those are completely normal changes. But it is important during these times to make sure you don't go totally over- or underboard when it comes to eating because this is when your bod needs nourishment most. Ideally, maintaining a balanced diet all year 'round is the greatest, but since we are human and have weaknesses for ice-cream sundaes and pop-corn at the movies, we're not expecting any miracles. It may seem impossible to eat three square meals a day—who has time?—but just making minor changes in your diet, like not having leftover birth-day cake for breakfast, can make a really big difference in your over-all health.

The foods we eat today are loaded with artificial chemicals, preserv-atives, and additives. Take a trip to your local supermarket and check out the aisles filled with fun foods that are ready to eat in 15 seconds flat. But hold on a minute. Anything that can sit on a shelf or in a vending machine for a year without spoiling is not exactly "of the earth." Cheese isn't supposed to come out of a can.

The hard part about becoming a choosier nosher is that the bad stuff's not always so easy to spot. You might know the obvious evils, like bacon double cheeseburgers, rich desserts, and fried foods, but a lot of the stuff we may think is okay has lots of hidden crap in it. Start reading the labels on packaged foods. If something has a long list of words you can't pronounce, put it back on the shelf.

Tougher to cut out are the foods we eat specifically for the kick they provide. Caffeine, the main ingredient in coffee drinks, soda, and chocolate, is a stimulant, which means it gives you a jolt. Each person is affected differently. Drinking lots of caffeinated beverages can make you jittery—not good for an already stressed-out teen.

The same goes for sugar. Yeah, we know it makes everything taste great. And if you're a person with a sweet tooth, you know how desperate you can be for a candy bar around 3 P.M. But sugar can be really bad when you eat too much. Like caffeine, sugar gives a burst of energy, but one that can leave you feeling even groggier than before because what goes up—your sugar level—must come down. And too much sugar can cause tooth decay, so brush those pearly whites!

Another crucial part of achieving overall health is exercise. Not only does it help keep your weight in check, but also it's a great way to offset the effects of stress. Exercising gets your whole body in motion, burning off those extra calories and the excess adrenaline your body is producing.

Keepin' It Real

"I started exercising a few years ago with my mom when she went on a diet. I was just doing it to keep her company, but I got in shape, too. I could see a difference in my muscles and stuff. I really felt good about myself."

—Alana, age 13

If you suck at sports and are way too uncoordinated to hit step class, there are plenty of ways to get your blood pumping. Splashing around a friend's pool, playing Frisbee at the beach, or running your dog around the block are all a-okay ways to get your heart rate going. Getting your groove on works, too. Turn up your favorite tunes and shake your thang. There are ways to work exercise into your life and have fun while doing it.

Now that you know how to be physically fabulous, we need to warn you about overdoing it. For guys, wanting to be more buff or make the weight requirement for a certain sport can load on the pressure. For girls, wanting to be popular and well-liked often means being thin. Girls and guys both want to be attractive to the opposite sex, but trying to drastically alter your body can lead any teen down a path of self-destruction. Some kids take dangerous measures to achieve their goals. With all the fad diets and quick weight-loss programs out there, we can get pretty caught up in just wanting to see results and not paying enough attention to what we are putting into our mouths. Chances are, any program that tells you to totally cut out certain basic foods or eat only one thing for a certain number of days is almost guaranteed to be unhealthy. Unless you have a severe weight problem, you can definitely find a smarter solution.

Anxiety Disorders

People who have trouble coping with stress may develop more serious conditions. Basically, anxiety is a state of constant nervousness and worry about everything under the sun. If grades, friends, your family, and your health are things that are always on your mind, it could be a sign that you aren't just stressed out, but plagued with something more serious. Anxiety manifests itself in a bunch of different ways, some being anxiety disorders.

Phobias

A person with phobias typically has a fear of a certain thing that really isn't dangerous. People can have a fear of almost anything. You may have heard of claustrophobia, which is a fear of enclosed spaces, like elevators. Others can be afraid of spiders, flying in airplanes, or even leaving their house. Any phobia can range from mild to severe.

Riding up 20 floors in a crowded elevator can make anyone jittery. But phobias become more serious when they start to affect your daily life. If you find yourself purposely avoiding situations or events that you know are normal things that someone your age should enjoy, you might want to consider talking to someone about your fears. These days, phobias can be successfully treated through therapy.

Panic/Anxiety Attacks

A panic attack can happen anytime, anywhere, and it comes on quickly with no real warning. A person having an attack may suddenly feel out of breath and shaky. The heart starts racing, and it feels like someone is sitting on your chest. A panic attack can last anywhere from a few minutes to a half-hour. Most people can remember feeling this way at least once in their life. Having a few episodes here and there is not cause for alarm, nor does it make you an anxious person necessarily. However, if you have regular attacks, you might want to get some help.

Keepin' It Real

"I had a panic attack right before getting on a plane to visit my grandma. I never flew by myself before, and I just started sweating really badly and getting kind of shaky. I couldn't breathe, and I thought I was going to die."

—Steven, age 14

Eating Disorders

Almost every teenager has been on a diet at some point. Even those of you with fabulous bods have become insecure once swimsuit season rolls around. The quest for perfection is evident in our society's obsession with physical beauty and thinness. But be careful—these things can come at a price.

In the worst-case scenario, becoming obsessed with how you look and how much you weigh can lead to a serious eating disorder. People with eating disorders generally have problems greater than just what they see in the mirror. They have emotional troubles, too, and are sometimes looking for a way to get some control over their life. They usually have low self-esteem and are tired of keeping up the appearance of being the "perfect" child.

Some people will starve themselves because they believe that they are too fat, no matter how much they weigh or what they look like. This is a self-image problem and has nothing to do with their true appearance or how others see them. They will refuse to eat, becoming thinner and thinner as time goes on, even to the point where you can see the bones of their elbows, knees, and ribs through their skin. By depriving yourself of the nutrients you need, you are weakening your entire body and doing permanent damage to vital organs. People with anorexia nervosa can suffer a bunch of different symptoms, including susceptibility to illness, loss of hair, loss of menstruation in girls, kidney trouble, and overall fatigue. You are even damaging your brain when you starve yourself. It needs food to work, and, by denying it, you are really asking for trouble. In the most severe cases, anorectics can starve themselves to death.

People suffering from bulimia nervosa, on the other hand, eat but then get rid of the food. Bulimics will often eat anything and everything in sight. They might down a whole pizza; wash it down with cake, cookies, and ice cream; and then go in the bathroom and throw it all up. Sometimes people with bulimia get rid of the "extra" calories by taking laxatives or exercising fanatically.

This cycle of behavior is abusive and very damaging to the body. It causes an imbalance in the body's blood and tissue. This can lead to tooth loss and bone density problems, and, in some cases, even death.

People with eating disorders may try to hide them from friends and family, but there are signs to look for. If your friend always disappears into the bathroom after your bagel-and-cream-cheese brunch, notice how long she stays in there. If your little sister pushes the food around her plate at dinner but barely eats anything, take note. Pay attention to how many times she says she's simply "not hungry."

These could be signs of an eating disorder. Help is available through counseling and therapy. But it's important to catch these problems early, before the physical damage to the body is too serious to repair.

Depression

Unfortunately, depression is an illness that affects lots of teens today. This is not just a case of the blues, but instead is a serious problem that can make a person feel like life is not worth living at all. Depression can be brought on by changes in life that are out of our control, like divorce, the death of a loved one, or being miserable at a new school. While you are expected—and allowed—to go through difficult times in your life, it's really important to get through them and move on. For people with depression, that can seem impossible. They feel defenseless against a slew of problems that have no apparent solutions, with no one to talk to and nowhere to turn. The worst thing about depression is feeling this way for a long period of time, in which a person loses the energy and creativity necessary to figure a way out of the funk.

Signs that you or someone you know is depressed include these:

- Lack of motivation
- Lethargy
- Change in eating or sleeping habits, either more or less than usual
- Withdrawal from friends and previously enjoyable activities
- Poor self-esteem
- A sense of hopelessness

Severe depression is accompanied by a feeling of despair and, in some cases, can lead to suicide. The feeling that a person will never be able to climb out of the black hole makes suicide seem like the only option. It is important for teens to realize, whether they are truly depressed or not, that the bad times don't last forever. There is a solution to every problem, although it is not always pleasant or easy to find. When problems start to mount and you feel like the world is crashing in around you, go get help.

Just because you are depressed doesn't necessarily mean that you will become suicidal. A depressed person may feel one or a few of these symptoms. Typically, someone who is suicidal will feel all those things all of the time. There is a way to get a grip on life, no matter what stage you're in. Counseling and therapy are terrific boosters. Realizing that you are not alone can be a great relief and enough motivation to want to heal yourself.

The Least You Need to Know

- Your mind operates your inner control panels when it comes to dealing with stress. You can't stop this process from happening, but you can learn how to deal with it better.

- The physical reactions that you can have to stress are uncomfortable, but they usually don't last.

- When stress leaves you feeling run down or overextended, your sleeping patterns can become disrupted.

- Maintaining health and fitness is a good way to ward off the more serious side effects of stress.

- Anxiety can cause a range of debilitating disorders that can keep you from doing simple, everyday activities.

- Depression is the ultimate mood zapper and even can lead to thoughts of suicide.

Pressure, Pressure Everywhere

The two places teens spend the majority of their waking hours are school and home—and both can be huge sources of stress. When one is bad, it makes the other worse. When both are on the rocks, look out—you're headed for a meltdown. Besides grades, which are a huge factor, you face lots of pressures at school. Your social life, your love life, and even your future life depend on how impressive you are during these four years. Trying desperately to fit in while maintaining a 4.0 can be exhausting, and the one place you look to for comfort and solace is your family.

Then what happens when your home life hits the skids? You are going to need to tap into a crucial resource: yourself. In the next two chapters, we'll discuss how a basic thing like going to school can get so complicated so fast, and what to do when your precious family unit feels some strains of its own.

School Dazed and Confused

In This Chapter

- Academic anxiety
- Athletes and attitudes
- The buddy system
- Love bites
- Educational hazards

School is not always the fulfilling and enlightening institution of higher learning we'd like it to be. Between classes, teams, and other students, something's bound to get screwed up and stress you out. In this chapter, we'll explore the aspects of school that can pummel you with pressure and why they can make you feel at your wits' end.

Class Struggles

High school is a hard thing to get through during a difficult time in your life. No one has an easy time of it, not even the kids you think are strolling through. The reality is, you have to spend a lot of time there, so you've got to try to make the best of it you can—and maybe actually leave having learned something. If you're smart about it, you can even learn to squeeze some fun out of it.

The major source of pain and suffering for many teens at school is classes. Even though they are the reason you're there in the first place, they often take a back seat to lots of other facets, whether social, romantic, or athletic. Since all these can be major stress causers, the academics often end up suffering. The performance of a stressed-out student wavers. He is easily distracted, tends to waste a lot of time, and gets less done than a calmer, more grounded student would.

Obviously, there are also many pressures that come from inside the classroom. This is a place where you're forced to sit still for hours at a time, listen to long, painful lectures, complete excruciating homework assignments, and then deal with exams. On top of it all, your highly competitive peers are just waiting for an opportunity to blow you out of the intellectual water. And sometimes, no matter how hard you try, you don't understand the stuff as well as the next guy. Hopefully you will have the good sense to get yourself some extra help, whether it's from the teach or a tutor. That could be the ammo you need to kick yourself up to better grade ground.

Competitive classrooms can be great at keeping you on top of your game. They can push you to achieve in ways you may never have on your own. But for all the good that overachiever students can accomplish, they can also get super-stressed over their grades. They may feel pressure from parents or teachers to always get great scores. They may also feel embarrassed in front of their peers if their scores are less than stellar or start to slide.

In direct contrast to this type of student is the teen who is shy about her intelligence. For some crazy reason, some kids don't think that being smart is cool. That's an off-the-wall concept since some of the most cool, powerful, admired people in the world are also brainiacs. Some smart teens would rather not answer a question in class that's a cinch for them. It's a shame to be embarrassed by a trait that should instill pride.

Living the Sporting Life

Are you a force on the field, a cougar on the court, a terror on the track? Then sports are probably a big, important part of your life. Sports are competitive by nature and demand aggression during the game, so naturally they can cause some stress. But that could be good for you. Athletic activity actually releases tension and provides a healthy outlet for all that energy of yours. Unfortunately, sometimes the stress is piled on athletes by outside factors and sometimes by issues inside their own heads.

There has been much controversy in recent years surrounding kids and organized sports. Excessive pressure is put on young athletes from parents and coaches. Some folks get way involved, watching every game, supporting the team, or maybe even practicing with their kid. Some coaches are really hard on the athletes, forcing them to work excessively hard and take the game really seriously. Come on, people! Isn't this supposed to be fun?!

Keepin' It Real

"I play soccer, and my dad comes to every game, even the away ones. I don't know what his deal is; it's not like he used to play or anything. I think he's just proud of me, which is cool. But he makes me so nervous. I play way better at practice when he's not there."

—Evan, age 14

Contrary to popular belief, winning in sports isn't everything. Too many people put way too much emphasis on that. Playing a sport just to smell victory is totally missing the point. There's lots of fun to be had and lots of great stuff to learn. By the way, effort and improvement count, as does the experience you can gain. So don't worry too much about collecting trophies. There are many great aspects of sports, but, realistically, it's not for everyone. Don't feel pressure to participate, and if you're already on a team and unhappy, quit. You're totally allowed. You should decide whether to play, regardless of what you think anyone else wants you to do.

Popular Science

One of the most fun things about school is that you get to see your friends every day. One of the least fun things about school is that you get to see your friends every day. Dealing with other teens is never easy. Some of them are nice, some are whatever, and others can make your life hell.

Things wouldn't be nearly as complicated if people didn't always have to break off into groups. Imagine if you could go to a school where everyone got along and everyone was appreciated for who they truly are inside. Now snap out of it 'cause it ain't never happenin'. Cliques and stereotypes are a fact of high school life. Even if you're not in a specific group, people feel the need to put you in a category and put a label on you. That's all fine and dandy, unless the label is hurtful. It can be silly, superficial, or a crock, but a lot of times it sticks. Girls especially have to deal with "reputations," even if they're not true. It's not fair, and it's a crappy position to be put in. Don't contribute to it. Don't assume stuff about others. Just because the girl in your psych class looks like a supermodel doesn't mean she's snotty. And the guy with the piercings and tattoos isn't necessarily a big, bad rebel. Take the time to get to know people before you make any snap judgments about them. You may look different, but you just may have more in common than you think.

Beware of Burnout

Sometimes you feel that you could lose your friends if you try to be too different or independent. A group of your peers can be a powerful entity. Take the high road, and stick to your gut when making decisions. It's your life, after all.

It's human nature to want to hang with people you have things in common with. It's fun to be part of a group, at this age when you're just figuring out who you are. The problem with this sort of closeness is when you're afraid to do your own thing apart from them. It can be majorly frustrating to feel like you can't really be your true self around your so-called "best" friends.

This is why the influence of peer pressure is so strong and so dangerous. You want to be liked and accepted by the other kids, especially the cool ones, but they may push you into doing things you don't want to do. It could be something like going to the mall when you don't feel like it. Or, things could get more serious. If your compadres start getting together to drink on the weekends, you'll probably feel pressure to pick up a beer yourself, even if you know your parentals would freak. And if your amigos started smoking pot, you might assume that you have to take a hit off their blunt just so you don't look like a goody-goody. You're totally being swayed by the group mentality.

You may give in just because you don't want it to be an issue. Sometimes you may put the pressure on yourself because you don't want to feel or look different. Trying to do your own thing often makes the clique feel rejected, like their way isn't good enough for you. They're trying, just like you, to feel confident. It sometimes helps people feel strong when others feel weak. As lame as that sounds, it happens and you may be a part of it.

The best way to protect yourself from the peer pressure trap is to have confidence in your own behavior. You don't have to be judgmental about what your pals are doing, but you also don't have to follow them around. It's good to have a plan ahead of time. Decide how you feel about important issues, like drugs, drinking, and even sex. That way, when confronted with them, you know how you will react and you'll be less likely to try something on a whim. Your friends' job is not to push you around and make you do stuff you're not into. If they don't understand that, maybe you're better off without them.

It's true there is something endlessly fascinating about the "cool kids," and wanting to fit in with them. The quest for popularity and coolness is one that some teens think will lead to a charmed life.

Not so. There are pressures on both sides of the fence. Some of the popular kids may be good-looking or more powerful in the school hallways. They may feel forced to act a certain way all the time. Some popular kids may totally abuse their power by bullying other students.

If you're one of those bullies, you'd better check yourself. Understand the power of words. Everything you say and do affects others. Teasing may seem like nothing to you, but to the person being teased, it could feel like a lot more. You could be the source of someone's stress. If you're the one being bugged or bullied, try to be cool about it. If you act like it's not bothering you, chances are, the jerk will get bored and quit it.

It may sound cliché, but the best thing you can do to keep out of the popularity struggle is to just worry about yourself. To gain respect from your peers, be a strong, assertive person. You can make people listen to you without being pushy and aggressive. Everyone is attracted to nice and outgoing people. Go out of your way to act that way. And expect it from others.

Fighting the Funk

Your friends should be kind and supportive and fun. They should relieve your stress, not cause it. If they're not cool to you, or they contribute to your insecurities, ditch them. You deserve better!

Friendly Fire

Fights with friends seem to happen a lot more lately than ever before. You're all so darn moody that it's easy to get mad at someone, or for your friend to get mad at you, if the wind changes direction. Fights with friends are majorly stressful. These are your peers, the ones who stand up for you and support you even when you're being lame. To lose them would be like losing a limb.

Keepin' It Real

"My friend Jana and I get in fights constantly. Over anything. I think it's because we're so the same. We always make up, though. I don't know what I'd do without her."

—Taylor, age 13

You're probably all so headstrong that it's hard to get someone to apologize, and without that, this thing could go on for days. Be the bigger person. Apologize and remedy the situation, if you have the power to. It's never easy since you're kind of laying yourself on the line. But nothing feels better than when a fight is smoothed over and you can go back to trying to crack each other up.

Because you're so tight with your friends, nothing stings more than betrayal. Maybe they said something about you behind your back, or they have something going with your honey. This is horribly painful, just ask Julius Caesar, whose best bud, Brutus, went and stabbed him. What a tool! Some friend he was. As hurtful as the situation is, the most you can do is to be up-front with the person. Don't hold stuff in; it will just keep your blood boiling.

Some friendships are just not meant to last forever. Breakups with friends can be difficult and awkward. One of you may feel rejected, or maybe guilty, and we all know how much that sucks. Try to handle the situation gracefully. Don't cause any further trouble; revenge is never a good idea. Try to be understanding and sensitive to the other. You don't have to be all dramatic, either. You can still be friendly even if you're not best friends. You're probably better off that way, anyway.

The Dynamics of Dating

Along with all this maturity and awareness comes another great awakening: the rumblings and grumblings of romantic interest.

Love and sex fill the thoughts of guys and girls alike. You can't help it, it's your biological programming. Romance can be one of the rockingest-walking-on-air feelings, but, like most things of greatness, it's usually accompanied by stress.

Even though you're in the throes of physical and mental turmoil during your teens, you're trying desperately to be suave. You wear your hottest, most dashing duds when you know you're going to be around potential cuties. But it's all about how you feel inside since that's what shines through. You wish for confidence and practice looking like you have it every chance you get.

If you're made of flesh and blood, you know all about crushes. You probably know why they're called "crushes," with all that aching they cause you. You feel like if you could just date that one person, you would be happy, happy, happy forever and ever.

Maybe you've gotten past the crush step to the actual dating phase. Maybe you've actually fallen in love. Well, congratulations. You've experienced what may be the most simultaneously beautiful and painful feeling in life. Love is so powerful that it's sometimes hard to tell if you're really in love with the person or just in love with being in love.

Dating is a big responsibility. You now have someone else's feelings and happiness in your hands as well as your own. It can be difficult, and so can your sweetie. They may even drive you nuts sometimes. But you deal with it because it hurts so good.

Rifts with your buds over who you date are a definite possibility. They may not love your honey nearly as much as you do. Your love might not dig your pals, either. It could be a personality conflict or just a jealousy thing about who you're spending your time with. Depending on how cool and liberal your school is, it could also be an issue for you to date someone of a different color, religion, or social class than you. What happens when you suspect that your sexual preference is different than what you assumed it was supposed to be?

Having a feeling, let alone coming to the conclusion, that you're homosexual or bisexual can be a difficult realization as a teen. Your attractions are different than what you were expecting them to be or what you were taught they should be. If your parents, friends, school, or religion are conservative, it can make it difficult, sometimes torturous, to be honest about who you really want to be with. This is one of the reasons why that darn "closet" is still so full.

It's a hard position to be in and a claustrophobic place to stay. Try to be as honest as possible, with yourself and with others. Use your best judgment in figuring out who to tell and how to tell them. If you're really uncomfortable spreading the word, or if you don't feel that they will understand, wait until you feel more ready. Admitting the truth to yourself is a terrific first step since you are who you should be concerned most with. After all, you deserve happiness in love as much as everyone else.

With all of this discussion around sex, what about the sex stuff itself? You've got these crazy, powerful urges like never before, and you can barely contain them. Are you even supposed to contain them? Whenever you get into a make-out session, it's all you can think about. Maybe you should do It. But it seems like these days, more and more people are going the classic route and waiting until they're older. Who's to say what's right for you?

Keepin' It Real

"My boyfriend and I were going out longer than all our friends ever did. For a long time, we just kissed and stuff. Then we did 'it' 'cause we thought we were supposed to. It changed everything and we broke up like pretty soon after that."

—Georgia, age 16

It's too bad there's no beginners' manual for sex. Who to do it with, when to do it, at what age and under what circumstances are you supposed to lose your virginity? You have to weigh all the pros and cons, both practical and philosophical, before you make a decision.

First, remember that sex is a huge physical responsibility. There's the threat of pregnancy, STDs, and HIV. If those are health issues you're sure you could handle, go for it. But if you value your life and don't feel like carrying a diaper bag to cheerleading practice, think twice. And if you go for it anyway, just make sure to use protection. You're a hip teen. You must know that already.

You probably have lots of other concerns, too. What will sex do to your relationship? What if you go for it, and then it's not even that great? It's not like it's gonna be hot and steamy like in the movies. It'll probably be all gropy and awkward. Not sexy. Sex can be wonderful and should be intimate. Love should be involved somehow, too. Just think long and hard before you take that roll in the hay. You don't get a second chance at having your first time.

Danger Zone

You're at school so much that it's kind of like a second home. An annoying, noisy home with gum stuck under the tables, but a home nonetheless. When you show up in the morning, you may be cranky, but you are supposed to be comfortable and safe. Nothing puts a damper on this cozy feeling more than a crappy school environment. Some schools are overcrowded and teachers are bored with their jobs, which makes them boring to listen to. Dangerous school hallways and the threat of kids bringing weapons to school can really put everyone on edge.

Feeling threatened at school seriously affects your performance. Your concentration wavers, and you are constantly stressed. Fear of a violent occurrence can be terrifying and even debilitating for teens. How can you possibly get your chem assignment done if you're nervous about something going down in the hallway after class?

Everyone is aware of the sad, scary stories being splashed all over headlines recently. Several violent instances in schools have made students afraid of their hallways and made parents fearful of sending their kids to an unsafe learning environment. This is a definite concern for high school students. But remember, these violent instances are still very rare. We've been hearing about them on the news, but they wouldn't be news if they happened all the time.

However, if you feel that there could be a serious threat, don't keep it to yourself. Maybe someone you know is teetering on the edge. Does someone carry a weapon? Does he say weird things and maybe even threaten to do something violent? Pay attention, and don't always assume that the person is just joking around. Use your judgment, and don't be over the top in your paranoia. You don't want to send a wave of panic through the school or get someone sent to the school psychologist just because he was having a bad day. But be aware of who and what is going on around you. If something seems fishy, mention it to someone, whether it's your parent or an administrator. In these cases, it's better to be safe than sorry.

The Least You Need to Know

- While the classroom is the place you feed your head, it can also be a competitive environment.

- Sports can release stress but also cause it. When it stops being a blast, just stop.

- Strong, healthy friendships are difficult to maintain, but they're worth it when they work.

- Sex and love are new concepts that you're just trying to figure out. Take it slow, and consider your options before you jump into a relationship, emotionally and physically.

- Instances of violence in schools are not common but can be scary. If someone is acting strange and you think he could break, tell someone.

Chapter 6

Harried at Home

In This Chapter

- Brotherly love
- Money matters
- Folks frenzy
- Worst-case scenarios

Let's face it, home is where the heart is. They may drive you crazy, but you can't help but love your kooky family. Heck, they're the people who have known you the longest and don't mind that you drool in your sleep and will only eat your peas if they're not touching your mashed potatoes. When the going gets rough at school or with your friends, you can usually count on your parents to be there for you. But what do you do when all of a sudden there's trouble in paradise? When something happens to shake up your family unit, it can be devastating for everyone. In this chapter, we're going to take a look at family dynamics, how they can stress you out, and how to alleviate the strain.

Sibling Static

Remember back to the good old days before your younger siblings were born? You were free to soak up all the attention, play with all the toys, and eat all the dessert. Then *they* came along, and nothing was ever the same. Let's face it, brothers and sisters are cute and cuddly at first, but they can really grow to be big pains in the you-know-what. They're always in your stuff, on the phone, or hogging the remote control. Then there's hoarding the last cupcake, breaking your CD player, wearing your favorite sweater, or eavesdropping on you and your friends.

Sibling rivalry is a whole different ballgame. Is your older brother a super-jock who's bound to get a college scholarship? Popular at school, a good student, and a hospital volunteer? Puke. Was your sister voted "most likely to succeed"? Was she dating the coolest senior in school? Did she submit the winning sculpture in the local art competition? How can you possibly measure up? Trying to keep up with someone who is constantly 10 steps ahead of you is exhausting.

So don't bother. If your big bro is a football hero but you suck at sports, don't sweat it. Do something you like instead. Explore your individuality. Usually our parents' pressure is meant to push us into excelling, not terrify us into failure. If Mom and Dad are pouring it on thick, let them know to back off; you are doing the best you can.

The same family rules apply with steps as when dealing with biological siblings. If your parents are fostering a competitive attitude, take a stand. You shouldn't be expected to be like anyone else but yourself. If you can't get along with a step-sibling, no matter how hard you try, that's a different matter. But it doesn't have to be tragic, so don't let it ruin your year. Some kids are like oil and water and just don't mix. If you truly gave the relationship a shot and it's not happening, you don't have to announce the revelation over pizza. Exercise your right to dislike someone in a polite, respectful manner. Sure, siblings can be annoying, but is it really so bad? There's always someone to talk to, someone to borrow clothes from, someone to share things with, or simply someone to blame when you spill grape juice on the carpet.

Financial Foibles

One of the great things about hanging out with our families is that we don't always have to act too-cool-for-the-room around them. Our classmates are not so forgiving. At school, everything's got to be perfect: your hair, your clothes, your jewelry, your sneakers. Keeping up with hot trends and styles is not only hard on your "fashion meter," but it can put a real squeeze on your wallet as well. The cost of coolness—new clothes, CDs, concert tickets, and movies—really adds up. The pressure to be like everyone else and able to afford new stuff all the time is very real.

But not everybody has enough spending money to keep riding in the fast lane. In fact, lots of kids have to take part-time jobs to help with family expenses. Money woes can have long-term effects, too. College is super-expensive, and not everyone can go to their top choice because of the cost. It's hard to listen to a classmate recount an awesome trip to the Bahamas when your family had a lean Christmas this year. So, what's a teen to do?

Keepin' It Real

"After my parents' divorce, there wasn't as much money to go around for allowance and stuff. I was mad because it was another way the divorce was changing my life for the worse. I ended up having to get a part-time job, and at first I hated it and was embarrassed to tell anybody. Then I made some friends there and we all started hanging out together. Having my own money also made me proud of myself."

—Samantha, age 17

Getting a part-time job is a start. Not only will you be earning your very own cash, but pulling off a very adult thing like a job shows that you can carry real responsibility. And if you can handle a job as a teenager, when you're also dealing with school and social stuff, chances are good that you will be able to tackle lots of the harder stuff that comes with adulthood.

If you know your family is having money problems, offer your support by suggesting that you don't need that new stereo or laser printer you've been asking for—at least, not right now. Mom will sure appreciate the fact that you're on her side. It's a safe bet that your parents are trying their best to provide everything, you need and the fact that they might be falling short hurts them way more than it does you.

The Parent Trap

If you're lucky, your family is your world, a source of comfort and stability. Home is the place where you can let loose and truly be yourself. But let's be real. There's no doubt that your family can stress you out. When Dad picks his nose while driving or Mom wipes your face in public, you want to crawl into a hole and hide. These actions not only damage your super-cool image, but they also are counterproductive to establishing your status as an autonomous individual. As annoying as these things are, there are more serious familial issues that may come up, making everyday embarrassing moments seem like a day at the beach. Life isn't perfect. Sometimes we have to face things that seem unbearable and get through things that seem impossible.

Divorce Doldrums

One of the scariest things in the world is the idea that our parents might not be together forever. We can sense when they aren't getting along. Sometimes the fighting is really bad, and it freaks you out. It may be a passing phase, or it can mean something more serious.

A lot of us can remember a time when our parents argued constantly. Maybe it felt like they started yelling at each other out of the blue one day and haven't stopped since. Maybe you've secretly overheard them for years, fighting in the next room when they thought you were asleep. You thought it was bad when they yelled at you, but it's far worse when all they do is yell at each other.

Lots of kids think they can help smooth things over by being a super-kid—you know, getting all A's in school and whizzing around the house with the vacuum. But getting voted class president or acing your piano recital is not going to change your parents' attitudes toward each other. Perfection is an impossible standard and not one that anyone should have to live up to. Chances are, you're a great kid and not the source of any of their problems.

Fighting the Funk

Trying to offset your parents' problems by being the perfect child won't help matters. You will only end up feeling run down and disappointed that your efforts were fruitless. Your parents' problems are strictly between them and are for them to handle.

Older kids might find themselves getting in the middle of fights between Mom and Dad. While it may be impossible to stay out of things totally, don't voluntarily try to mediate an argument. Parents' fights are often about issues that are between them and that have nothing to do with their children. Sure, they might be arguing over who should drive you to your friend's house, but that doesn't mean you should stay home to eliminate a sore spot. They are really disagreeing about something different altogether.

Regardless of the scenario, we never expect our worst fears to come true, but sometimes it does: the big D ... divorce. Life as you know it will never be the same, but it doesn't have to be miserable, either. A lot of times, divorce can mean a new beginning—and an end to all the fighting. At least you don't have to walk on eggshells anymore wondering when the next outburst will be. Living in a tense household can really work your nerves, and you may find yourself distracted at school or overly sensitive when hanging with even your best of friends. Although it will take a toll on the entire family (even Fido feels the strain), divorce is something you can get through and still love and be loved by both your parents.

Keepin' It Real

"I was so scared when my parents said they were getting a divorce. I hated them both for a while. After it happened, though, I had to admit it was nice to live in a house that was quiet, without all that fighting over stupid stuff. I was able to relax more."

—Katie, age 13

A tough lesson we all learn in growing up is that our parents aren't perfect human beings. They make mistakes and get upset and throw things. Sometimes they act exactly the way they tell us not to. It's important for kids to remember that they are not responsible for what's going on during these tumultuous times. This is a tough thing to accept as a kid and an even tougher thing to actually deal with. Seeing Mom cry or Dad storm off after dinner is just awful. You feel helpless and alone, and, worst of all, if they're upset, who's going to hold your hand through all this? It's a very complicated situation, and you are not crazy for wanting to throw a tantrum or lock yourself in your room for a hundred years.

After parents split, living in a single-parent family requires some getting used to. Pressures come from having new responsibilities around the house or baby-sitting a little sis or bro. You might end up cooking dinner nights Mom has to work late or occasionally doing a load of laundry. Not only are these additional chores a big downer, but helping out around the house also means less personal time for you.

This new lifestyle may feel weird at first, but having a positive attitude about it will help. Mom and Dad are going through a really rough time of their own, and being a trooper will make them eternally grateful. Don't let things get out of hand, though. If you feel that too much responsibility is weighing you down, or if you're worried about a parent, spill the beans to them. Sometimes when a kid approaches a parent about stuff, it makes the parent feel better. They need to talk about stuff, too, but are sometimes afraid that they're only adding to your burden. Communication is always great, and it keeps everyone on the same page. The situation is probably not as bad as you think.

Family Fault Lines

The issue of custody is another doozy that needs to be settled. More than likely, a kid's time will be split between both parents. All these changes can make a person feel as if he's in constant motion. Weekends with Dad, holidays with Mom, back with Dad for birthdays. Having two bedrooms, two toothbrushes, and a weekly commute is enough to drive anyone batty. If it helps, keep a schedule. Write stuff down in a book, or post a big calendar on the fridge. This will help everyone organize their lives. Eventually things will settle down into a routine.

Think you can relax now that you've got the 411 on divorce? Not so fast. Once you've gotten used to your new routine as a super-solo commuter teenager, parents can throw another curveball your way—the dating scene. Not yours, theirs.

Ew. You've barely figured out how to attract the opposite sex yourself, and now the thought of your mom going on a date is grosser than gross. Parents aren't supposed to dress sexy or hold hands in the movies. That's your job. Dating among the sweater-vest set is definitely weird and hard for teens to get used to.

Creepier than the possibility of your dad having a girlfriend before you do is the idea that he'll actually marry her. You finally got used to the divorce scenario, and now there's a third party thrown into the mix. Being introduced to a parent's romantic partner is strange, uncomfortable, and embarrassing. Where do step-parents fit in, anyway? They're strangers you're supposed to be friends with but also obey. Sound confusing? That's just the tip of the iceberg.

Sharing a parent that you already feel you kind of lost in a divorce can be a really tough thing to face. But before you declare war on your parent's new love, ask yourself how much quality time they're really stealing from you. Probably not much. Think about the positives: Now you have another person to go to your plays, help with homework, and chauffeur you around. Hmm. Can't hurt, right? Remember that the newcomer is struggling, too. It's a whole new world for a step-parent who has just inherited an entire family. But if the idea of cozying up to someone new is really upsetting you, take things slowly. No one expects you to become an instant family; all they're asking is for you to make an effort.

Once you do, you might find that you really like your new insta-parent. Of course, this can make a kid feel stressed, too. Hitting it off with a step-parent might make you feel guilty, like you're leaving your biological one in the dust. The bottom line is, there is always room to love another person in your life. When families grow, whether it is the birth of a baby or the addition of step-family members, so does the capacity for love and happiness.

Keepin' It Real

"When my Dad first introduced me to his girlfriend, I thought she was pretty and really nice. She didn't mind seeing the movies I wanted, and she was a really good cook. I pretty much liked her right away, which I totally didn't expect."

—Jerome, age 14

With new family ties often come new living arrangements. Moving into a new house or apartment can be traumatic. For example, you know you're totally too old for a security blanket, but your house can kind of represent the same thing. Houses are filled with reassuring memories that you're not necessarily ready to give up. You know exactly where the floor squeaks in the living room so that you can avoid it when sneaking in late. Your bedroom is your sanctuary, and you aren't ready to pack it all into a cardboard box. Unfortunately, you don't get much of a say in these situations. So look at it this way: Moving can be a time of opportunity and a chance for a new beginning and a fresh start.

Moving to a new neighborhood, city, or state, however, makes things more complicated. Relocating your CD collection down the street is one thing, but hauling butt to a whole new town and school is enough to make the stress monster rear its ugly head. Now you're also living the universal nightmare of being the new kid in school. Don't expect to make new best friends the first day. But be brave and introduce yourself. Keep cool. After what you've already been through, this will be cake.

When Bad Things Happen to Good People

Some teens face different family issues altogether. Not everyone has loving and supportive parents, whether they are married or divorced. Some parents are dealing with big problems—emotional, physical, or financial—of their own and find it difficult to help their kids navigate their way through adolescence.

Having a parent with a substance abuse problem can be a real dilemma that a teen can't handle alone. Adults in this situation are not acting responsibly. Worst of all, they put their kids' well-being at risk when they aren't sober. A less attentive parent means that more responsibility falls on the shoulders of the child. Sometimes it adds to violence in the home. There is no excuse for physical or verbal abuse. Whether it is committed by parents, step-parents, relatives, or anyone else, a kid never deserves it, no matter what anyone says.

Growing up is hard enough to do without having to constantly worry about these huge issues. The tough thing about fixing these situations—and they can be fixed—is that asking for help is hard. Just admitting that there's a problem can be embarrassing for everyone involved.

But help is available. A trustworthy relative or teacher might have some good advice or, better yet, might offer immediate help. Explain what's going on and that you are scared, embarrassed, and afraid. There is a solution, and you can deal with your family's problems with dignity and privacy.

Beware of Burnout

A teen should never have to deal with serious problems alone. It can be dangerous, and you need outside help. Talk to an adult you trust, and tell him what you are going through. This is the first step in helping everybody.

Dealing with the illness or death of a parent or sibling can wreak havoc on even the strongest of families. We are never prepared for it, and it can leave us feeling a lot of mixed emotions: guilt, loss, and even anger at the person for dying and leaving us all alone. Our feelings don't always make sense, but they are very real and you may feel like you're dealing with them on your own. The other adults in your life are coping with their own pain and might not be ready to handle yours as well.

It's important at times like this not to try to hide your feelings in order to be strong for others. This will only hinder your own healing process, and no one wants you to suffer any longer than you have to. Allow yourself to grieve. Talk about your pain with relatives who offer support, and, if necessary, take some time off from school. Everyone will understand. The sooner you face the pain, the sooner you will be able to get on with your life.

Our families may not be perfect, but they are our flesh and blood, and they mean the world to us. When the rocky times hit, it's crucial to try to stick together and offer support wherever it's needed. Be the best daughter, son, sister, brother, grandkid, nephew, or niece that you can be, and the effort will be appreciated.

The Least You Need to Know

- Getting along with siblings is not always easy to do, but it's important to try.

- Not everyone is lucky enough to have unlimited spending money. Feeling like you can't keep up with what your peers have or where they're going on weekends can make you feel like a big loser.

- Major life changes like divorce and remarriage affect the whole family and require that everyone make an effort to understand and cooperate.

- Don't hide your feelings inside or retreat to your room when major issues strike. Talk about them instead and you'll work through them.

Taming Tension: Fighting the Fire with Force

By now you know what stress is, where it comes from, and what it does to your mind and body. Now let's get to the good stuff. You need info on how to beat stress and make sure it doesn't rear its ugly head around these parts again.

In the final six chapters, you will learn some great ways to deal with outside pressures and make sure you're not accidentally adding any yourself. Don't forget to take control of your own life and never let it go. Loosening your firm grip will only compound your problems. So get ready to get clued in on lots of great tips, advice, and strategies that will keep the stress monster at bay.

Chapter 7

Finding A Fine Timeline

In This Chapter

- You're only young once
- So much to do, so little time
- Finding focus, and fast
- Busting bad habits

You're a teen on the go, and you like it like that. Your life is packed to the brim; you work hard and play hard. It is a very fulfilling way to live because you are trying to suck the marrow out of every second. But sometimes your schedule seems too full. You're running yourself ragged and don't know how to put the brakes on. You don't have to let an overly busy schedule stress you out. You just need to start managing your time better. In this chapter, we'll take a look at how hectic things can get and ways to break the frantic cycle.

Juggling an Active Lifestyle

You're a new millennium teen, and you've got it going on. Actually, you've got *everything* going on, 24/7. You're busy constantly because

you have to be. How else are you going to do that you want to do—
or that you have to do? Besides, it's fun to be a teen, and you want
to get the most out of it. You have goals, darn it!

There's never a shortage of ways to spend your time these days.
The number of potential activities seems endless. All these things
take time and energy. You're young, you can handle it. But should
you? You have to decide for yourself what you want to fill your time
with.

School automatically takes up a big chunk of your day. At least you
wake up every morning and know where you need to be. But just as
you drag yourself out of bed, you remember that extra-credit homework assignment you completely forgot about but that you absolutely need to do. You scramble to write something down and then
rub your lucky rabbit's foot, hoping that you didn't completely
screw it up. You can't afford to not get the credit since you're already teetering on the precipice of a really pathetic grade in the
class. Now it's late, and you're afraid you'll miss the bus, so you
grab a half-frozen waffle and run out the door ... then run back in
to kiss Mom goodbye (she gets mad when you forget that) ... and
then out again.

Once you get to school, you rush to your locker to grab your books
and then jet to drop off the extra credit to your teacher. Mission accomplished. Now you've got to get to class, where you have to sit
still for more minutes than you'd like. Yuck.

Keepin' It Real

"Lots of mornings I'm too busy to eat much
breakfast. I usually wake up late and maybe
have to finish some homework. I just grab a granola
bar or something before I go. I don't know why I do it
since those mornings not eating makes me even more
tired."

—Julie, age 15

And you can't really just sit there, you have to perform—and perform well. Okay, focus. Focus. It's hard since you're mind is all over the place and you're still kind of tired. You raise your hand once in a while to show the teacher you're paying attention, when what you really want to do is talk to your friends, pass notes, or gossip. You want to vent to them since you're also stressing about the school dance in two weeks, for which you remain dateless.

In a moment of spaciness, you don't notice your pen roll off your desk. Before you know it, the cutie next to you has picked it up and handed it to you. Awww! Note to self: Find some time to talk to Cutie re: dance date potential. It's not long before your mind drifts to a bunch of other things, like school assignments, an upcoming party, and a favor your dad asked you for that you need to think about or deal with. You'd rather be getting started on one of those things, but instead you need to sit in this chair. Total drag. Aaaah! You scream in your head and wait for the next bell. By lunchtime, you're finally kind of awake and happy for the break, even if it's a temporary one.

But it's not really much of a break, is it? You head to the cafeteria to grab something to scarf since you're starving. Pizza today. Yum. You down a couple of slices and then skip out because you have an emergency yearbook meeting or student council meeting, or maybe you just have to meet one of your buds in the courtyard to discuss his crisis-of-the-moment. Your friends need your genius words of wisdom because you're the only one who they really trust with whatever their problem is. So you head over because you're a good yearbook staff member/class secretary/friend, even though your hands are greasy from the pizza, you dropped sauce on your shirt, and you really want to try to talk to Cutie to start laying the groundwork for going to the dance together.

You fulfill your lunchtime obligations, then head off to finish your afternoon classes. Finally, it's the last class of the day and you start to feel like you can breathe again. Just before you leave class, the teacher assigns a book report due next week. Great.

You jam because you have soccer practice, or you have to baby-sit your little cousin, or you have to get to your after-school job at the record store. After a few hours, you rush home for dinner with the family, which you're already late for, because your folks want to "eat together like a civilized family." You chow your meatloaf, dodge your parents' questions about your "mystery" date for the dance, try not to get in a fight with your bro or sis, and then escape to your room, which is not really an escape, since you have a couple hours of homework to do. By the time you're done, you're beat but need to unwind, so you blab on the phone, surf the Net, or play video games. Finally, you collapse into bed. Better get some sleep because you have to wake up in the morning and do it all over again.

When Having It All Is Way Too Much

Talk about full days! That's all you ever have anymore. You long for the old times, when childhood days seemed long and lazy. Now that you're a teen, the days often go by super-fast because you're so busy.

School classes and homework are more than enough to keep you occupied, especially if you want to do well in them. And if your classes are challenging, forgetaboutit. Total time-eater. Between the hours you put in at school and the hours you (should) put in after, you barely have space for anything else. But if you want to have a life, you make time for it, even if that means your schoolwork sometimes suffers.

Then there are the other school and community activities, clubs, groups, or sports teams. Meetings and practices and games can take up hours and hours, especially if you're really involved. And who wants to do something halfway? If you're going to be involved, you try to give 100 percent.

And there's the fun stuff, which can sometimes be less than fun: your social life. Friends and significant others take up lots of your time. You want to hang out and have fun as much as possible. But along with the good comes the less-than-good. To keep relationships going smoothly, you've got to work hard. But you have trouble finding time to deal with your own stuff. Add in the hours you get stuck dealing with friends' problems, and the time is just sucked away.

Beware of Burnout

We sometimes look for excitement in relationships and situations, and we create it when it's not there. Be careful of friends who wrap you up in their drama. It can end up taking up lots of your time, forcing you to neglect your own business.

To top it all off, everyone has some kind of family obligations to deal with. You want to go with your friends to a football game on Sunday? Forget it. You'll be grounded 'til graduation if you skip Great Aunt Edna's birthday party at the roller rink. Gotta finish that book report? You'll have to do it after you're done mowing the lawn, which you promised to do during one of your sweeter moments.

No matter how completely lame they seem to you, your folks still have the power to make your life miserable. So you play with your little sister like Dad wants you to, even though you feel like cutting her pigtails off like she did to the doll you got her for Christmas. Your mind is racing, and there are a jillion things you'd rather be/should be/need to be doing.

You feel pulled in all different directions when all you want is to sit still for a minute. But there's no time for that. People expect things from you, and you want to deliver because you don't want to let anyone down. That is a commendable attitude to have. It's an amazing trait and not a very common one, so take a second to gloat.

Now that you feel all warm and fuzzy, think about how your active lifestyle makes you feel. Are you nervous all the time? Claustrophobic? Feeling never good enough? Maybe all of the above. If you're super-busy and constantly on the move, you probably also feel at the mercy of your schedule. There never seems to be enough time for everything. Time can be stifling. It can make you feel tense and freaked out at the possibility of never being able to get everything done. It's all fine and dandy to have a full schedule and a full life, but only if you feel like it's worth it. If you spend too much of your time trying to do it all, you may end up doing the opposite. Running yourself ragged can eventually lead to burnout, which will only make the situation worse.

Keepin' It Real

"I used to be really involved at school. I was on varsity softball, in lots of clubs. I also do really well in classes, but only because I work hard at it. Finally I just got completely annoyed with everything. It was just too much. I had no time to do anything fun anymore."

—Carrie, age 15

In your attempt to fit everything in, you might be taking time away from places you need it. Some teens sleep or eat less in order to have time to get more done, which is obviously totally unhealthy. Some let schoolwork go to spend more time on social stuff, or they start dissing friends to get schoolwork done. And when was the last time you took some time for yourself? Before you know it, you're living your life for other people. You're at the mercy of all these activities that just keep taking up your time and threatening your sanity. If you don't regain control of your time and achieve some balance in your life, you're eventually going to crash. And you'll open your eyes and realize that you're not even living your own life anymore.

Trimming the Fat

Getting your life in order does not have to be a traumatizing experience, so don't just put it on your already full list of "things to do." It can be easily accomplished if you want to make the change and alter some bad habits. Life is chaotic, it's true, but you may be totally exacerbating the problem by mismanaging your time.

We're all guilty of that sometimes. You know you have stuff that needs to get done, but other things come up and you find yourself distracted. You spend too much time on some things or not enough on others. Activities can take longer than you expected, and, before you know it, the whole day gets away from you.

You can't always predict how smoothly things are going to go or how long they will take. But plenty of time is wasted because of poor planning or a too-jumbled schedule, or procrastination, or sometimes laziness. You can take control by improving your habits. You'll be surprised at how much smoother life can be with just a little forethought and some wise decisions.

To figure out how to best use your time, you must first be reminded of a fact that you already know but that you're probably in denial about: *You cannot do it all.* Literally there is no way humanly possible for you to be involved in everything. There are only 24 hours in a day, and you are only one person. When you have too much on your plate, there's not enough time to do anything properly.

So, the first step in cleaning up your schedule is to prioritize your interests and activities. Think about all the stuff you spend your time on. Some of it you need to do, like schoolwork and probably familial obligations. But there's lots of time left that you're filling with other things. Think about what those activities are, and ask yourself some questions:

- Which do you really enjoy?
- Which do you get the most out of?
- Which are helping you get closer to your goals?
- Which do you feel are essential?
- Which are you better off without?

Chances are, you spend precious time on things you're not that interested in. Maybe you stuck with them out of habit because people expect it of you or because your friends are involved. If these activities are not working for you and are eating up lots of time, think about cutting them from your schedule.

Once you figure out what you really want to spend your time on, be committed to those activities. Be the best at them that you can be. Don't just do a half-baked job. Throw yourself into whatever you're doing, and go for it. If you love your job at the ice cream parlor, make the best darn banana split around. If you like being a reporter for the school newspaper, work on becoming an editor, too, and stay involved in the most intense way you can. When you're focused and really try your best, your confidence and self-esteem will skyrocket, and you'll feel like a rock star.

The way to keep it all together is to be organized. Okay, so not all of us are the "organized type." Your room may look postapocalyptic, but that doesn't mean the rest of your life has to be a mess. If you know you have lots of things to do and they're all just floating around your noggin, get them out of there by writing them down. Make lists of what you need or want to accomplish. This will help you organize your thoughts, too. And they will seem like less of a big deal when you can actually look at what needs to be done.

Keepin' It Real

"I have to write everything down. I'm like the king of list making. But I have to be-cause, even if I don't have a lot to do, if I don't write it down, I'm a stress case. It's way easier to deal with when I keep it in order."

—Billy, age 16

Next, prioritize your list. That way the most important stuff gets done when it needs to, and less important stuff, like "buy new Smelly Angels CD," gets put off for a while. It's not always as much fun, since the Smelly Angels rock, but you'll feel so much better knowing you're on top of everything rather than under it.

It's also a good idea to consider when your best performance times of the day are, or when you're really "on." If you're a morning person, schedule stuff earlier. But if you don't really get with it until later, do the easy stuff first. Then by the time you're really ready, you'll be able to better handle the more challenging parts of your schedule.

As you do things on the list, cross them off. And don't feel bad if you don't finish everything. The list is not carved in stone; it is only a guideline to keep you on track. You don't have to be overly ambitious, making monster lists that are too hard to tackle. Set small goals and then set off to accomplish them one step at a time. This will save you from panic and that terrible stress of feeling overwhelmed.

Some times are definitely busier than others. One week you'll have 10 tests, your best friend's birthday party, and Granny coming to visit. Then the next week, you'll have nothing. It's a good idea to figure out your schedule by actually making a schedule. Get yourself a calendar and fill it up so that you can keep track of every meeting, practice, party, test, due date, and family dinner at the local buffet. You can keep your head together if you keep organized. And plan on things taking longer to accomplish than you think they will. Often complications come up, activities run overtime, and you're thrown completely off schedule. But with good planning you'll be better able to deal with it.

Fighting the Funk

Without a planned schedule, events have a tendency to sneak up on you, which can cause major stress. If you have your day or week planned ahead, you'll be better prepared to handle upcoming stuff.

Planning Pitfalls

All this planning and organizing can be totally undermined by certain bad habits, like procrastination. If this is one of your weaknesses, you've probably become pretty creative when trying to avoid doing something you don't want to do. You don't feel like building that model of the universe out of golf balls for science class, so suddenly you feel the need to brush your poodle, pick fuzz off all your sweaters, and see if you can name all 50 states in alphabetical order. Basically, you're wasting time, and you'll pay for it later. You may get the assignment done eventually, but if you wait until the last minute, you'll be totally stressed and then end up doing a crappy rush job on it. Sometimes, if your schedule is too full, you don't feel like doing anything at all and you tend to put everything off, which only complicates the situation. Talk about feeling like a prisoner of the clock! But you imprison yourself, and you suffer for it.

It's a bad habit, so break it. There will always be things you have to do that you don't want to do, but putting them off does not make them go away. Stay away from the TV and the computer, too. Both of these things have the amazing power of sucking away precious hours that are never to be seen again. Keep track of your time. Wear a watch, and don't let time get away from you without a fight.

Another sticky trap is saying "yes" to everything that is asked of you. You want to be a good person and a good friend to all your buds. Sometimes that just means hanging out when they ask you to, and other times it means doing them favors, both of which can be time-consuming. Be careful not to spread yourself too thin by being the "yes-friend." Of course, you want to have fun with them and be reliable and trustworthy, the one everyone can count on. But don't forget to be a good friend to yourself, too.

Sometimes you need to say "no" to others, even if you don't want to. Know your limits, and then draw the line. Pay attention and take note if you ever feel like the time you spend with or on your friends could or should be used better on your own stuff. Start turning down invitations, and think twice before you agree to do a favor. It doesn't mean you're a bad, flaky, or lazy friend. It just means that you acknowledge when you don't have the time or energy to do the job well. It's your life that's getting too hectic, not theirs. So you need to take the reigns and put a stop to friends robbing you of precious moments.

If something is stressing you out, reduce the time you spend on it. (Unless, of course, it's an important, necessary thing. Then you'll probably end up spending more time on it.) If you're on the debate team because you know that colleges like to see it on your transcript, fine. But if the mere thought of public speaking makes you so nervous that you feel like you're gonna hurl before every debate, you should seriously consider quitting. Nothing is worth that kind of stress. No *one* is, either. If you have a friend whose habits stress you out, like partying too hard or even just driving like a maniac, consider cutting the time you spend with that person.

It's your life, and you need to spend it in the way that's best for you. You don't always need to be on a schedule, either. Sometimes it's good to forget the schedule altogether and just l-i-v-e. Do stuff you want to do, like hobbies that you may have gotten too busy for. And keep some time empty so that you can fill it however you want. You're a teenager, after all, and you're entitled to have the time of your life. Don't forget, you're also allowed to be spontaneous. And remember to save some time to breathe!

The Least You Need to Know

- Between school, family, and friends, your schedule is often a whirlwind of responsibilities that you struggle to meet.

- Overextending yourself can lead to burnout, which will throw a wrench in the active life you want to lead.

- Taking control of your schedule, and your time will allow you to lead a more fun and more productive life.

- Try to reduce wasted time by changing a few bad habits, like procrastination and over-commitment.

Chapter 8

Taking It Down a Notch

In This Chapter

- Ticked-off teens
- From 0 to 60
- Beyond the boiling point
- Steering clear of the red zone

Sometimes your fuse is shorter than others. Something will happen to just set you off, and before you know it, your temper gets the best of you. You're angry and not in the mood to apologize for it. It's not one of your favorite feelings. Actually, it makes you pretty miserable, but it sometimes seems like you just can't help it. Well, you can. In this chapter, we'll explore the anger emotion, what triggers it, and how you can learn to control it and stop letting it control you.

Anger, Angst, and Aggravation

For most teens, life is not a bowl of cherries, a box of chocolates, or anything even mildly sweet most of the time. Often a bowl of mold or a box of cockroaches is a more fitting description of the way you view the world and what happens in it. It's a rough bunch of years for all concerned, with all those physical and emotional changes that are taking place. A lot of what you are dealing with at home, at school, and with friends can really bug you. Usually these are just mild irritations, but sometimes you feel really pushed to the limit. Stuff digs right in and hits you where it hurts. You get edgy. You get annoyed. You get angry.

Anger can be caused by a variety of situations. Maybe you open the fridge to discover that you're out of milk and have to eat your Sugar Snappies dry. Or you need to do your math homework in pencil, but you just broke the point of the last pencil you can find in the house and realize that you left your sharpener at school. You finally get home after a long, traumatic day of pop quizzes and lunchtime gossip desperate to call your new sweetie, only to find your big sis totally hogging the line. None of these things is the hugest deal, but any one of them can be annoying and can leave you teetering on the edge of some less than sparkly feelings.

The Great Frustration Frenzy happens constantly, and it happens to the best of us. Like, no matter how much you study, you just can't seem to break your C streak in geometry. Or maybe you need to re-search an assignment online, but every time you find what you need, your screen freezes. These types of situations that feel out of your control can really work your nerves. It's like some weird cosmic force is sabotaging your efforts. No one likes to fail, even at small stuff, especially when really making the effort to succeed.

Keepin' It Real

"I decided I wanted to learn how to play guitar, but I just couldn't get it. I thought I'd be wailing some Hendrix song in, like, a week. Not a chance. I couldn't even play a chord. I almost threw the thing through the window."

—Parker, age 15

Unfortunately, anger is not an emotion we grow out of. Everyone gets angry sometimes, it's unavoidable. Like stress itself, it's a response you feel that is not necessarily good or bad; it just depends on how you handle it. But if everyone supposedly feels it, why do some people never seem to show it? They're always pretty calm and collected, even when the going gets rough. If they are subject to the same daily frustrations you are, how do they stay so darn calm? The difference is in their approach to things. They react in a more mellow, laid-back, and rational way.

On the opposite end of the spectrum, some people tend to fly off the handle at even the slightest bump in the road. We're talkin' over something petty, like when the batteries go out in the remote control. But if these are both very real examples of reactions, how do we learn where it's appropriate to draw the line? Anger is a tricky feeling to cope with, but it's totally manageable, as long as you have the desire and the know-how to learn to chill out when the mercury rises.

Why are people's responses are so different? Well, because people are so different. The first and most obvious reason is personality. Some folks just naturally have short tempers, while others are pretty low-key most of the time. But other factors come into play, too, like cultural differences and a person's level of self-esteem. Men and women respond to stress differently. Some religions are based on developing inner peace and control, so, as a general rule, their followers tend to take adversity in stride. Confident people tend to be calmer since they view situations more objectively and get less upset over things out of their control. Age is also a factor since younger people who are just beginning to learn how to control their tempers may lose it over smaller things that wouldn't bother someone a little older.

Experience can also really affect the way a person reacts to angry feelings. Witnessing or experiencing an injustice can easily bring someone to the boiling point. Experiencing or witnessing any type of prejudice might lead you to develop a "hot button" that makes you more aware of and sensitive to that type of situation in the future.

If you're wondering where you get your anger response from, take a look at your family, since that's who you learn from. Are your parents yellers? Do you have to wear earplugs in the car when Mom gets mad at Dad for not asking for directions? Maybe that's why you tend to raise your voice when your baby brother messes with your stuff.

Keepin' It Real

"Everyone in my family talks in really loud voices all the time. I do, too. I have to, or no one will hear me. When we get in fights, we all yell. When me and my friend got in a fight one time, I was really mad, so I was yelling, and she was just talking in a normal voice. I didn't even notice until she said something."

—Katie, age 13

As you grow up, you're becoming more aware and concerned with fairness. Because of what you were taught as a kid, you came to understand that there was an order to the world, right was different (and better) than wrong, and things happened the way they should if you were a good person. But it wasn't long before you learned that life doesn't always go the way it's supposed to. Life is not always fair. When you were little, maybe you got grounded for fighting with your brother, even though he totally started it. Today such an injustice is still a part of your life, and this can get the anger pumping through those veins.

Since anger is another one of those primal caveman responses, it can also be caused by threats to your safety or brushes with danger. It's another one of those trusty defense mechanisms designed to protect you from harm. Being hurt physically or emotionally will spark an angry response. In an attempt to protect yourself, loved ones, or anything else you feel worthy, your anger gauge may end up in the red zone.

But besides threatening outside forces, you can cause your own thermometer to rise. Sometimes you're being bugged by what's happening in your own head. There may be stuff coming up in your life that's got you totally stressed and wracked with worry. The more you think about it, the more intense your negative feelings get. Sometimes past memories of fights with friends or nasty gossip that went around about you can dredge up hostile feelings as intense as when the incident first went down. Although they are in the past, you just can't seem to let them go.

Beware of Burnout

Don't automatically feel guilty about feeling angry. It's just a natural response to some of the less pleasant sides of life. Fortunately, it can be controlled—and it can even be helpful when handled properly.

Anger gets a bad rap, even though it can be a catalyst for positive change and actually can be quite constructive. When something goes awry, your body gets prepared to react. It's like a red light starts blinking inside you as a warning to get ready for action. Feeling angry may push you to solve a problem that you might have otherwise let slide. It is a passionate feeling that may spark in you the desire to fix something that is broken or to right what you feel is wrong. If a rule or policy at school that you strongly disagree with makes you angry, it may lead you to take steps to make a change where you think is necessary.

Anger has actually led to great accomplishments and positive change throughout history. Just look back at social changes that have occurred in the good ol' U.S. of A., and you're bound to see that they were made as a result of someone, or a lot of someones, getting really peeved. Whether the subject was racial inequality, the inability for women to vote, or fur as a fashion statement, people got angry and then took action to fix the situation. Charities have been started, political movements have been inspired, and environmental foundations have been established, all thanks to passion and anger over the way something in society was being handled.

But while anger can give people the shove they need to make good things happen, it can also lead to destruction. To a great extent, anger is damaging and can be harmful to personal relationships. Serious, biting anger can drive people to seek revenge, which is always a terrible idea. In the worst, most dangerous scenarios, anger can lead to violence against oneself or to others, and can also be a step toward trouble with the law.

Now that we know there are different ways people deal with their anger, let's see where you fit in. Say that you're supposed to meet your bud for a Saturday matinee at the mall multiplex, but he's a total no-show. Later, when you finally get him on the phone, he admits that he got totally sucked into his favorite video game, Super Rocket Skunk, and lost track of time. To top it off, he's not even acting like he did anything wrong. Now you're super-pissed. You …

a. Don't push it and just let it slide. If he doesn't think it's a big deal, there's no way you're letting on that you do. Who wants to sound desperate?

b. Start yelling and yammering about what a miserable little skunk *he* is.

c. Act like it's no big deal but then tell him that you can't drive him to the party tomorrow night. That'll show him.

d. Get your feelings out. Tell him that it bugs you when he's a giant flaky flake, and he needs to not waste your time making you wait around for nothing. Please.

If you answered a., you probably deal with your anger passively and tend to not really show that you're pissed at all. Did you pick b.? Then you're an aggressive one who leans toward extreme reactions, like yelling or exploding when you're angry. You c. kids out there are probably the passive-aggressive type. Your immediate response is fairly calm, but you'll let your anger come out when you find a less direct way to attack. The d.'s have the most rational response of the group. They deal with anger assertively, and they like to express their feelings and talk things out. No matter how you respond to your anger, you can always change it and learn to deal in a more healthy, more constructive, and less destructive way. Stay tuned, and we'll give you some pointers on how.

Spanning the Spectrum

No one knows you better than you. You probably have an idea what your own anger patterns are like, what types of things upset you, and how much. However, you may also have noticed that you rarely respond the same way twice to a situation.

Anger levels can vary greatly. You might get annoyed over something small and then get sideswiped an hour later because something else totally throws you for a loop, hurling you into the rage zone. Since it's impossible to predict future events and how you'll feel at that time, it's also impossible to predict your reactions.

It's hard to put a finger on what's going to set you off—and to what extent—because the stuff that triggers you is constantly changing. The things that burn you up inside today may not be the same things that would have a month ago or that will two weeks from now. Your feelings and thoughts about the world around you are constantly changing. Every day you are having new experiences; you're reading and learning more. Naturally, all that affects the way you think and feel about things. It just shows how easy it is to change what bothers you. It's another aspect of your life that you can take control of if you choose to. And you should.

Lashing Out

We all experience anger, sometimes more often than we'd like. And sometimes anger may rise to levels we wish it wouldn't. Anger, like most emotions, can be exaggerated by a variety of outside forces. If other aspects of life are out of control, amounts of anger and the way they are expressed may get that way, too.

Physical or emotional abuse can cause anger levels to career out of control. A bad situation at home or with a boyfriend or girlfriend causes such chaos that the rest of your life becomes just as much of a mess. The black cloud covers much more than just the incident in which the abuse occurs. Its effects can be far-reaching and disastrous.

Constant stress may also lead to uncontrollable anger. When the pressure is always on, it's hard to remember what life was like without it. It stays in the back of your mind all the time, keeping you on edge and ready to explode at even the slightest thing. Continuous stress is not necessarily due to a busy schedule. It can be a result of environment, like living in a noisy neighborhood. If you live in a bustling big city, you probably know what we mean. The continuous sounds of traffic, babies crying, kids playing, and sirens can really get to you, especially if they never let up. People who live in environments like this may be so used to it that they don't even notice it. But the din is there, day and night. It has a constant stressful effect, not allowing the human brain the moments of silence it needs to function smoothly. It's easy to shut off the TV, but not to turn off the world around you.

A traumatic experience can also be the cause of extreme anger, as can a chronic illness. These things can be so upsetting that they never seem to leave the consciousness of the person and can be at the root of serious bouts with anger. In addition, drug use or a mental disorder can cause someone to display anger in an extreme, irrational way.

Out-of-control rage can be a scary thing. Certain signs distinguish a person in this danger zone from one who simply has a short fuse. The person whose crossed the line may have high levels of anxiety. He may lose interest in stuff that he used to like. As with other kinds of stress, sometimes a person struggling with anger will have difficulty sleeping or eating. The quality of performance at school or in other activities can decline. People who are struggling with anger may also start to act out, in an effort to release some of the pressure they feel inside.

Don't Get Mad, Get Glad

Whether you are a rager, a door-slammer, or one of those people who just *thinks* curse words when something ticks you off, there are ways to alter the way you manage your anger. You can't control the world around you or predict what's going to go down that will throw a wrench in your plans. But what you *can* control is just as important. You can control what makes you angry and how angry you get.

As we mentioned before, teenagers are at one of the most volatile times in their lives. You're moody, you're emotional, and you don't like to take crap from anybody. Some of you may deal with this stuff in a violent way. You may have already been in a fistfight or two. And at the time, you probably thought you had good reason to throw some punches.

Keepin' It Real

"I was always kind of a tough kid in my class. No one really messed with me, but sometimes something would make me mad and I'd pick a fight, just 'cause I could. I'd beat up some kid for no good reason. It was stupid and mean. I feel really bad whenever I think about it. I would never do anything like that now."

—Steven, age 14

Hopefully, you realize that's kid stuff. Scrapping is something you do before you know better. And you should know better by now. Hint, hint. If talking with your fists is still part of your language, take a second to be embarrassed, and then silently make a pact with yourself to never do it again. Come on … you're a bigger, better, smarter person than that. Mature people know how to deal with their anger. They can force themselves to keep calm, even if they initially feel like lashing out. They can control themselves, their thoughts, and their actions. And you can, too.

Sure, anger sometimes feels like something that's happening *to* you, something that you can't help. This is because it is a physical response. When faced with the thing or the threat that makes you angry, your body releases hormones, including adrenaline, to prep you for dealing. This happens in different amounts according to the size of the threat. You need to find a way to deal with the hormone surge. You need a release. This is what the phrase "get your aggressions out" is referring to. Physical activity definitely helps here; all cultures have sports or war as ways to exercise their anger out. If you're the furthest thing from a jock, sports may be the furthest thing from your mind. So do something else, like sprinting around your block. If you have to, punch your bed pillow. You'll be amazed at how much calmer you feel after just a little bit of physical exertion.

Fighting the Funk

Growing up and older will help you battle anger as well. Most people chill as they age. Think about how your grandparents behave. There's probably a totally relaxed vibe about them. They may get cranky, but they're usually way more mellow than you. So hang in there, and you'll eventually get more relaxed, too.

Now you know a little more about how to deal when the anger bug bites, but there are ways to rip out the negative feelings by their roots and attack the problem at its core. It helps to be a little self-evaluative about this. Consider your own personal response to what angers you. What types of situations tend to really rile you up? Do you feel like your parents nag you way more than they do your siblings? Is there someone at school who you consider your archnemesis? Some super-villain whose every move just drives you up a wall? Are you ultracompetitive on the playing field, so much so that the mere thought of losing makes your blood boil?

Certain people, things, issues, and situations push our anger buttons. Think about what those are—make a list, if there are several.

Then evaluate why you think they happen. What are those reasons? There might be a simple explanation, and one that you can possibly get to the bottom of. Maybe you're the only girl in a family of boys. Your folks may "nag" you out of concern or overprotectiveness. Did that kid at school who you can't stand ever do anything to you personally? The more you understand what makes you angry, the easier it will be for you to figure out how to steer clear of potentially troublesome situations. Your anger may have always gotten the best of you pretty quickly, and it's possible that you never looked deeper to try to understand where these feelings really came from.

Unfortunately, no matter how hard you try to avoid potentially volatile situations, once in a while you will inevitably find yourself smack dab in the middle of one.

Before you move a muscle, take a deep breath and concentrate on staying calm. Count to 10, if you have to; just bring it down a notch. Be quiet for a second and think about the situation at hand, and try to keep a level head about it. Your car got hit, but it really only got a tiny scratch, and you have insurance. Yeah you have mud on your jeans, but you actually have a pair of track pants in your locker that you can easily wear for the day. It's that moment the hot-blooded anger first strikes that is the most dangerous. That's when people get themselves into trouble. They act out of the anger without considering the situation or the consequences of their words or actions first.

Think about what it would take to solve the problem. Maybe you're better off ignoring it and walking away completely. A confrontation is not always the best idea. But if the situation involves another person, you two can totally solve it calmly if you work it out in a smart way. Talk it out. Every problem has a solution; you just need to find one that works for both of you. This often takes some compromise, so be ready to bend a bit.

When in a conflict with someone, listen to what the other person has to say, and learn what the issue is. Try not to place blame, even if you feel that it's totally the other person's fault. If you start accusing people, they will immediately get defensive. One way to avoid this is by talking about how *you* feel (use "I") rather than what someone else did (stay away from the word "you"). Don't say, "You suck"—say, "I think it sucked when ...." And if the other person's dealing with it like a total nut, be the cool one and rise above it. You're too good to mudsling, so don't let this get to you. If a one-on-one discussion is just never going to clear up a heated argument, try bringing in a mediator, someone subjective, to help you sort it out. In some situations, two people will never see eye to eye and must agree to disagree. Having a rational head will help preserve your own sanity and your relationships with others as well.

These tactics on how to keep cool may not work for everybody. If you get angry easily and can't figure out how to control it, you need to get help. Speaking to a counselor or a therapist can be the best thing. They can help you find out what's behind your behavior and will then be able to better teach you how to cope with your anger.

Life is always going to bug you. Situations will frustrate you, and people will annoy you. But you don't have to be at the mercy of your emotions. Take responsibility for the way you handle your anger. Learning to change your reactions and chill out will make you a more grounded, cooler person throughout the game of life.

The Least You Need to Know

- Anger is a defense mechanism that helps prepare you to deal with a threat.

- The stuff that triggers your anger is constantly changing, just as you are.

- Uncontrollable anger can be caused by traumatic or seriously frustrating situations, such as abuse, trauma, or illness.

- You can control what makes you angry and the level you feel it.

Chapter 9

Be a Control Freak

In This Chapter

- Tough love
- Prioritizing principles
- Bird's eye view
- The world is your oyster

Conquering stress has a lot to do with your outlook, attitude, and perspective. Besides channeling positive thoughts, you can improve your chances of success in life by changing some bad behaviors. The ways you handle situations and deal with conflict are good indicators of your stress-busting abilities. In this chapter, you'll learn how breaking a few simple habits and improving your self-esteem will put you on the path to beating stress at its own game.

Doormat Don'ts

Chances are, there's a girl or guy at school who walks down the halls like he or she owns the place. Some people seem to have a natural strut that just oozes cool and sends the message: "Don't mess with me." How do they do it? They may have been tipped off that confidence and self-esteem are way important factors in maintaining a healthy and positive self-image. People who possess these traits carry themselves with a confidence that commands respect. How we view ourselves in many ways determines how others will treat us.

You don't have to just watch other people sparkle. You can do it, too. By having a good sense of who you are and what you believe in, and a grasp of right and wrong, everyday questions and dilemmas can be much easier to face. Being confident is not about being perfect. It's about making firm decisions that are right for you. Developing these aspects of your personality will enable you to handle the random and rapid-fire problems and choices that are constantly hurled at you.

However, these characteristics don't come easy; you might need some guidance. You've probably heard some people described as being "doormats" or pushovers—you know, people who let others walk all over them. It's important to be kind to people, but that doesn't mean letting them take advantage of you. Unfortunately, there is a fine line between being nice and doing doormat duty. There is such a thing as being *too* nice.

Keepin' It Real

"When I first started high school, I was always offering to do things for people because I thought it would make them like me. I didn't know a lot of people then, and I thought that would help me make friends faster. Now when I think back, I just get embarrassed that I tried so hard."

—Rebecca, age 15

For instance, are you the one who ends up driving your crew to the mall every Saturday? Is your big brother always mooching off your allowance money because he blows his on stupid stuff and then doesn't have enough to go to the movies? Did you lend your history notes to the hottie who has only shown up for class once, just 'cause you couldn't resist those baby blues? You could be borderline push-over.

The need to belong and feel accepted can get the better of anyone. From small things, like loaning sweaters and CDs that never seem to get returned, to bigger things, like drinking or doing drugs, it's important to learn to put your foot down once in a while. It's easy to just go with the flow or be swayed by friends to do something we aren't wild about or know our parents would disown us for. Being easygoing and flexible are really great qualities to have, but not when it means doing things that go against your personal prefer-ences and better judgment. When it comes down to it, only you know what's best for you. Don't be intimated by people you think are cooler, smarter, better athletes, or hipper dressers.

Let's say that two girls you know from gym class announce that they're cutting third period and invite you to go with them. You have a math test third period and know that you seriously risk flunking the class if you bail. You're not exactly a goody two-shoes, but it's too big of a risk for you to cut. You like these girls, though, and want them to like you. Dilemma. You decide that you can't do it, but now what do you say? It would be wildly uncool to hem and haw in front of the dynamic duo. You don't need to make a scene or insist that they follow your moral high road to make your point. Bow out gracefully and go about your business. Avoid feeling like a giant awkward dork by not sticking around to hear everyone's protests. And it doesn't hurt to have a sense of humor when dealing with these kinds of situations, either. People tend to let you off the hook if they're laughing. Keep in mind that everything you do has consequences, and getting in trouble for something you weren't re-ally even into in the first place sucks big-time.

Some kids think they can win popularity by being overly generous, offering rides around town or swims in their pool, or letting class-mates cheat off their tests. Exchanging material things for friend-ship is never a good bargain. People who just hang around with you for what you can give or what you can do for them are not your true friends. You can't invent chemistry between people—in friend-ship or romance. Good relationships have nothing to do with material possessions. If you know someone who is always offering to do things for other people, be the bigger person and don't take advantage of them if you know that they only want attention.

Fighting the Funk

Be your own biggest fan. Feeling good about yourself will give you the confidence to make decisions based on what's best for you, not everyone else.

With so many dominating forces in your life, you are bound to get your wires crossed with people at some point. With parents, friends, your job, schoolwork, and other commitments, it's only a matter of time before you show up at the dentist wearing your football uniform or forget to pick up the dog at the vet. Oops. Miscommunication leads to lots of fights and misunderstandings, but it doesn't mean that you're the only one at fault or that you deserve the brunt of the blame. It's especially important when the mix-ups are more serious. If you've ever been accused of plagiarizing a book report, hitting your sibling, or flirting with a friend's honey when you were, in fact, totally innocent—you know the horrible feeling. Defending yourself against unfair accusations by teachers, friends, or parents is your total right. Don't take the blame for something that you didn't do. It isn't fair, and you don't deserve to take the fall.

You can keep yourself from falling into the doormat trap by learning to be assertive. It will not only help avoid being taken advantage of by others, but it also can help you seize new opportunities. You might never become an extrovert, but you can learn to stand up for yourself.

Being proactive is another way to make things happen for you. Don't just take what life throws your way. People who are afraid to speak up or who are afraid of being teased let themselves fade into the background and often don't get what they want. Don't let that happen to you. If you want something, go after it. Don't wait for someone to pick up on your vibe or make assumptions about your interests—guess what? They're too busy thinking about their own thing to notice yours. No one can read your mind. Ask out that cute guy in your homeroom that you've been eyeing the entire year. He might have been hoping you'd make the first move.

Whether it's initiating dates or running for student government, don't be afraid to make yourself heard. Push for things that are important to you, and don't take "no" for an answer. It might not always work, but it's amazing how good it feels to stand up for yourself and speak your mind. You know that you have a lot to say.

Control Yo'self

Just as it's important to know when to say when to others, it's necessary to learn how to put the brakes on yourself. One of the biggest parts of becoming an adult is learning to practice self-control. You may not have noticed, but you've already done it millions of times. Self-control means not throwing a fit when your little brother lines his hamster cage with your vintage comic book collection. It means not hauling off and punching that dude in chemistry when he points out that you smell like sulfur—in front of the whole class. And, on a bigger scale, it means learning how to prioritize your life, set goals for yourself, and sometimes put off until tomorrow what you want to do today.

Self-control can be more complicated than just getting a grip on your temper. It also means making greater sacrifices now in order to see bigger results later. A good example of this is saving money from a part-time job now so that you are able to afford to go to a better college when the time comes, or studying extra hard for an exam that you know will count for a big part of your grade. By thinking ahead, you are developing a *muy importante* skill: long-term planning.

It's hard to deny yourself things now in the name of an uncertain event in the future, but if you practice this kind of thinking when you're young, it can really give you an edge throughout your life. Changing course now so that down the road you can be more successful is a survival skill that helps people accomplish great things, like earning a college degree, buying a house, and having the career of their dreams. Being willing to put time and effort into reaching your goals is a very adult thing to do, and it makes your accomplishments that much more satisfying in the end.

Keepin' It Real

"Even though I was dying to go on this ski trip with all my friends my senior year, I knew I needed that money for a new computer. It was a really tough decision, but I decided not to go. I did feel bad when everyone was away and I wasn't, but I knew I wanted the computer more."

—Jackie, age 17

One of the most important decisions a teen will make is when to have sex, if at all. If you have a boyfriend or girlfriend you really care about, this can be especially difficult. This decision belongs to the individual alone and should not be influenced by anyone else's opinion except your own. Even if you think you're ready, holding out on something like sex until you feel even more comfortable with yourself and educated about the consequences can mean the difference between having a so-so experience and a fantastic one. The bottom line is, there are lots of things you can do and say in the heat of a moment or because it brings you instant pleasure. But taking the time to put even more effort into things can make all the difference in the long run.

Personal Perspective

With all the talk about how you can be the greatest source of your own stress, it's important to remind you that you also possess a stress-busting super-power. We mentioned in the beginning of this chapter that the way you look at things can be very effective in reducing how stressed out you get. Your perspective on life, and your opinion of yourself, is ultra-important because it can turn overwhelmingly bad situations into totally deal-able ones.

Unhappy people tend to compound their problems by having a negative outlook on life. Small setbacks do not necessarily have to amount to giant obstacles. If your significant other of two weeks breaks up with you, it does not mean that you're going to end up an old, lonely cat owner. By adjusting your focus from the negative to the positive, you will see the world through a much rosier lens.

It can be hard to put a positive spin on certain things. Getting fired from your job or denting the bumper on the family truckster are hard things to sugarcoat, but it is possible to find a silver lining. Instead of repeating "This always happens to me" 10 times in our head, you can squeeze a little bit of positivity out of it just by changing your attitude. If you got fired, now you can get a more interesting job that you actually like doing. If you banged up the car practicing your three-point turns, be thankful that it wasn't your dad's new, midlife-crisis sports car. You might be paying for that until retirement, but a dent is no biggie. Get the drift?

Beware of Burnout

A bad attitude only makes things worse. The more negative you are, the more likely you are to stay in a slump. Break the cycle by deciding not to let everything get you down. Changing your outlook to the sunnier side makes the future look way brighter. If you can't convince yourself to truly cheer up, just try pretending for a while and see how it feels.

Sometimes what can keep you from having a more positive attitude is a knack for reliving moments in the past. Nothing can stop a positive thought in its tracks faster than the image you have of yourself screwing something up. Going over and over past mistakes in your mind keeps you from feeling confident about the future—a trap we all fall into once in a while. Examining why a situation or conversation went wrong can help avoid a repeat performance, but dwelling on it can be paralyzing. Just because you stammered all the way through your first oral report doesn't mean that you will do it the second time around. With a little prep time, you can change the course of events. Practice in front of the mirror, put on your lucky shirt, and give 'em everything you've got.

Confronting fears and insecurities can be very empowering. If you do it enough, it can give you the feeling that you can do anything. When you are able to take disappointments in stride, you will no longer get so stressed out by setbacks.

Things don't always work the way you want, no matter how hard you try, so when a plan goes bust, don't beat yourself up over it. When you do accomplish something, go ahead and pat yourself on the back. You deserve it. Learning to appreciate and acknowledge your finer qualities is crucial to developing a high self-esteem. A great self-image is what will make you a force to be reckoned with in life and help the bad stuff roll off you like a cheap sweater.

Getting Comfy in the Driver's Seat

Once you've adopted the take-no-prisoners attitude, it's up to you to keep the ball rolling. Being consistent in your new role as ruler of your kingdom is important. Remember, control the things you can, and take the rest in stride. Once you get the hang of it, it will be hard to imagine life before your super-duper attitude adjustment.

Be creative in your approach to problem solving. Not every situation is black and white. Being open-minded opens up a whole slew of possible solutions to things. Turn a problem over in your mind. By using your imagination, you can create solutions no one has thought of before. And never listen to anyone who says you can't do something. There are ways to achieve the impossible. If you have faith in yourself, you can prove 'em wrong.

Even though you might not have a say in the structure of your life, you can decide how you are going to tackle the things within your reach. At school you have to take certain classes, and, chances are, you must be a part of a social scene. At home, some rules and circumstances were made and created without your brilliant input.

You may not agree with the way your parents handled a family situation, and you can't necessarily change their opinion or reverse their actions. But you also don't have to follow in their footsteps. Pretty soon you will be making your own decisions, and the more you pay attention and think about things now, the more confidence you'll have in your choices later.

The same goes for school. Wearing trendy clothes or listening to music that the cool kids like if it's not your cup of java will just make you tense and weary. Being phony takes a lot more effort than being honest. You can't necessarily change what others consider ideal, but you don't have to follow them, either. Do your own thing, but be prepared. Being unique usually means going against the grain. Doing things differently or expressing unpopular ideas may sacrifice your social standing a little bit or even get you strange looks in the halls. But allowing others to dictate the way you live your life is the uncoolest move of all.

Imagine that all your friends have decided to go bungee-jumping this weekend and, of course, assume you're in. Okay, looking at this from all angles, you come up with three very real "cons." First, you're afraid of heights. Second, you'd rather not spend the $50 it would cost since you're saving up for a DVD player. Third, your parents would pass out if they knew.

You decline the invite, saying that you have to baby-sit for your little sister. No point in admitting that looking down from a stepladder makes you want to toss your cookies. On Monday, however, the news circulating the halls is that the weekend excursion was a blast, everyone took the plunge, no one got hurt, and they even met a professional stuntman while they were there. "Darn," you think to yourself. "I shouldn't have been such a wimp and should have just gone, too."

Wrong-o. You weren't a wimp. You decided that what everyone else was doing wasn't for you. What if you had gone, thrown up in midair, and been a laughingstock for the rest of your high school career? Or, you could have gone, jumped, and felt great about it until you got home to find out that your parents saw the whole thing on the news because that professional stuntman was there with a TV crew. Ouch.

Only you know your true feelings and unique set of circumstances. Making a decision based on what you think is best for you at the time means that you took charge of a situation and didn't just follow everyone else. Sometimes that may mean missing out on something fun or exciting, but you take the chance with every decision that it might not be the right one. However, you'll never regret having been in control of your life. Next time you may choose another option, but as long as you maintain control, you won't be disappointed.

You can control certain elements of your life with a little character development and some careful planning. The world wasn't built in a day, and you can't change overnight, either. Set goals for yourself that are realistic and achievable. And then revel in each small success. Each step is a victory in its own right and just pushes you toward—and over—life's big hurdles.

The Least You Need to Know

- One of the first steps in taking control of your life is to not let yourself be pushed around by others.

- Being in control of your own actions and making thoughtful decisions leads to greater personal satisfaction.

- The way you view things in life can greatly affect how stressed you become on a daily basis. A person's ability to make the best of a bad situation is crucial for long-term success.

- Life is what you make it. Get used to the idea of controlling your destiny.

Chapter 10

Decisions, Decisions, Decisions

In This Chapter

- It's your choice, so make it
- Problem solving with panache
- Your conscience, your guide
- Toughing it out

Each day consists of a long string of decisions that are up to you to make. Even though it feels like adults make a lot of choices for you, you still decide whether to follow those. Too bad these decisions are not always cake to make. With so many roads to choose from, it's difficult to know which are the right ones for you. In this chapter, we'll evaluate the decision-making process and explain how a little know-how can keep your stress level down and your success rate up.

What's Your Problem?

Every time you turn around, you're being bombarded by a constant stream of questions, decisions, and problems that you need to handle. Funny how you never really noticed them before, but now they're looming around you, begging for your attention. Some of this stuff is easier to deal with than others, but sometimes it feels like the simplest issues can leave you baffled.

Teenagers are infamous for being wracked with indecision. On one hand, you feel like you know everything. You're a big-shot big-kid now, and you're the master of your domain (even if that domain consists of only a pretty shrimpy bedroom and half of a school locker). But, at the same time, you also think of yourself as a clueless little kid, totally confused and a little freaked out by the scary, mean world that makes you want to hide under your bed with your old, ratty security blanky.

Sorry to say, you can't hide forever. Toss off those covers, and fold blanky and put him in the closet. You're smart, you're capable, and you're growing up. When faced with a bull, you have to take it by the horns. When faced with a problem, you have to solve it. When faced with a decision, you have to make it. Be an active choice-maker, not a passive one. The more flaky you are in the process, the more you risk an end result that you won't be thrilled with.

Okay, so maybe making consistently quick, smart, great decisions is easier said than done. Big stuff, like choosing what college to go to, is obviously nothing to scoff at. But small stuff, like which flavor drink box you feel like having, can often leave you just as stupefied. That feeling of being swamped by the matter at hand can be incredibly stressful. When you don't know what to do, you tend to worry even more, which, as we all know, can get way out of control and does nothing to remedy the situation. Letting yourself be overcome with worry can lead to a helpless, hopeless state of mind.

To avoid that drowning feeling when confronted with a problem, it helps to fully understand what you're dealing with. Take a long, hard look at the situation and get to the core of it. The meat and potatoes are what you need to conquer. It's important to resist the temptation to put Band-Aids on a bigger problem, even though that would be easier than handling the whole shebang. You need to be honest with yourself when you check out the scene, even if the truth is hard to face.

Sometimes it's not so easy to find the source of a problem. And when things snowball, they become more complicated because the core trouble gets hidden deeper and deeper. If your grades are slipping in Spanish class, it may be because you're not studying enough. But why aren't you putting in the time you used to? Is it because your recent breakup with Shmoopy has gotten you down? Or maybe you're spending a lot of time hanging with a new group of friends. Either way, that is the core, the real reason your grades are spiraling. It's completely within your control to fix. You decide how long to mourn the loss of your romantic relationship, or how much you hang with the kids. By deciding and then changing the cause, you'll be changing the effect, and your grades will pick up again.

Keepin' It Real

"When I started high school, I knew I couldn't play both soccer and football anymore. I had to pick one, and I had no idea what I should do. I put it off so long that I missed the first practice of both of them. I finally picked soccer, and it's cool. I really like the other kids on the team."

—Steven, age 14

Decision making can be a bummer if you don't know which avenue to choose, but it's especially so if you don't like any of the choices. Unfortunately, most decisions that come up don't go away. They linger until you handle them. Denying that they're there or avoiding them altogether only postpones the inevitable. It's the wimpy way to handle stuff, and you don't want to be *that* person. Get your strength together—you know you have it in you. Then jump in, take the plunge, and make the decision. It's the only way to make it go away. The issue is then off your plate, regardless of the outcome of your choice. It's like ripping off a Band-Aid, which is never as painful as you think it'll be. Once you get used to handling choices in a proactive way, you'll get better and better at it. You'll begin to have a handle on stuff that would have seemed daunting or even impossible to you before.

Keeping a clear head helps immensely in these matters. When you're feeling overwhelmed, you often look at things with a cloudy, warped perception. Being irrational only exaggerates your stress and can make the simplest decisions seem complicated. Steak or chicken? Chocolate or cherry? Loose-fit or boot-cut? If you're one of those people who freaks over minutia, you need to get a grip. These are not earth-shattering events, so don't treat them like they are. Unlike bigger, more important decisions, they will have very little, if any, long-term effects. So flip a coin, if you have to, or carry a magic eight ball around; do whatever you need to do to make a quick pick and save yourself the stress. Heaven knows, you're feeling enough from other places.

The teen years are the first time you're actually getting to enjoy some independence. It's a blessing and a curse, since you want to be independent so badly but you feel torn about it. You're comfortable being dependent on Mom and Dad. It's warm and safe, and you understand your role in the family. Besides, a lot of the hard stuff is handled by them, so you, as the kid, can just cruise along, for the most part. The thought of breaking away from the nest is appealing, since you are getting a little stir crazy at home, but it's also kind of scary.

So what if you want to cut the apron strings, but your folks hid the scissors? Plenty of parents have a difficult time letting go of their precious babies. They still think of you as an innocent toddler, without a clue about life or the world. Handle them gently—they're only parents. They love you and want what's best for you, but they may not realize how sophisticated you really are. To show them that you're capable of looking out for yourself, prove it by making smart, well-thought-out decisions on your own. When they see that you have a good head on your shoulders, they'll be more apt to let you stray a little farther from the tribe.

Parents and authority figures make some decisions for you; you don't have much choice in the matter. Your peers, however, have no business sticking their nose in your issues. If you depend on them for making your decisions or let them influence you, they will continue to do so. It's also more likely that you'll end up doing stuff you don't want to do. So speak up. Make your own choices and solve your own problems. After all, you alone have to deal with the consequences. And only you know what's best for you.

Love It When a Plan Comes Together

We would all love to be the type of person who knows exactly the right thing to do at the right time. You know the kind: These people swoop into even the most horrendous hurricane of a situation and then, with wisdom and grace, mend the problem by effortlessly making all the right decisions. Do they know some magic wand dealer and are hoarding his phone number? Could be, but maybe they have just figured out a good system of decision making and they know how to execute it.

As we mentioned before, if you are faced with a big, ugly, complicated task, it often helps to dissect it first. Smaller parts are easier to tackle. Once you start dealing with these, you begin to chip away at the monster. It won't be long before you're wondering why the task initially seemed so daunting.

Let's say that your two best friends get in a huge fight at a party where lots of horrible things were said, and they swore to never talk to each other again. You know that this current battle is only the culmination of a million little incidents between them lately. You take it upon yourself to step in to try to smooth things out, since it's in your best interest to solve this. Their fighting would make your life miserable. It takes about a week, but you go from one to the other, explaining the other's side on various smaller issues and trying to get them to stop being mad about all those little things. It was all those tiny problems that led to the huge one, but once you worked those out, that big mean stuff from the party starts to become less of a big deal.

Fighting the Funk

When approaching a situation, it's important to keep focused on the problem at hand. First, figure out what your goal is. Then make your decision based on what you think it would take to accomplish that. Fixate yourself on the prize, and then do what you need to do to achieve it.

It's easy to get distracted from your main goal, even if you're trying your darndest to concentrate on it. Some situations are difficult to keep in order in your head. From different angles, certain decisions may appear easier or more logical. Try to look through all that mush and keep sight of what you ultimately want to achieve through making this decision. This method works with situations of all sizes, whether you're trying to decide which pair of sneakers to buy or who to ask to the prom.

Gather all the info that relates to your decision, and you will be way more prepared to make the best choice. Then consider the consequences of each of the choices. If you buy the more expensive track shoes, they'll last longer and will give you better support when you go jogging in the mornings, even though the other pair is cheaper and cooler-looking. Going to the prom with Billi would be a total blast. Andy is really sweet but quiet. Remind yourself of your goal and then consider the consequences of the choices.

In the process of considering your choices, it is also helpful to recall any experience you've had that relates to the issue at hand. And it doesn't even have to be something that you personally went through. You may recall something that a friend experienced or that your cousin did. Maybe your Mom told you a story that was kind of similar to the situation you're faced with now. And don't laugh, but, chances are, you saw some TV character deal with a related event at one time or another. Even if these "experiences" aren't exactly like what you're dealing with, they may shed a different light on the subject. They may remind you of the way you do or don't want to handle the decision.

After you've collected all your info and have thoroughly evaluated your choices, it's time for the moment you've been waiting for: You must make a plan. If your head is spinning with facts, write them down. A simple list of pros and cons can lay out the deck so you can see all the cards clearly. Then figure out the best method and execute it. You may be nervous, especially if there's a lot riding on this. But remember, stalling will not make it go away or make it any easier.

When you finally make your decision, stand firmly behind it and stick to it. If you've taken the time to consider the facts, you will have made the best decision you possibly could. You made a smart move, whether it turns out to be the right one or not. After you've buzzed in with your answer, be satisfied with it and do not mull it over and over in your head. Your move has been made, and there's no sense in turning back.

Beware of Burnout

Some problems are extremely difficult to solve and may even seem impossible. These will take the most effort on your part. They take dedication and persistence. But you'll be fine. You've got plenty of both.

In trying to solve a difficult problem, you may truly feel that your method of handling it may not be the best one. In these cases, it helps to have a backup plan in mind. Consider what may go wrong, and think of how you could swoop in and save the situation at the last minute. Your Plan B may end up being the glue you need to fix things.

Moral Mysteries

A whole crop of situations that you encounter in life have no black or white solutions. Sometimes the line between what you want to do and what you should do is so blurred that it's hard to see how either way will work at all. Moral dilemmas can often leave you confused, frustrated, and clueless as to how to handle them. We often find ourselves smack dab in the middle of unpleasant situations that we are forced, through no fault of our own, to deal with. Sometimes you're pulled onto these rocky roads by a least-likely villain: your buddy, your pal, your friend.

Friends make up your "other family." They understand you better than anyone else, and you'd pretty much rather hang out with them than anyone on Earth, with the exception of a few very cute rock stars. But what do you do when your friend starts to walk a path that's different than the one you want to walk? One that's darker and smells like trouble …. Just because you two are like two peas in a pod most of the time doesn't mean that you think and act the same all the time. The stuff your friend starts getting into might be questionable and something you're not really into. It could be something hard core, like drugs or stealing, or something closer to home, like purposely disobeying your parents' rules. Regardless of the size of the issue, it will be up to you to decide how to handle it.

It's a really tough situation to be in. You and your bud have been through a lot, and she may feel like a sister to you. How are you expected to go against her in any way? Maybe she's starting to develop a bit of a wild side. She's hanging out with a faster crowd and staying out really late on the weekends, sneaking home stealthily so that her parents don't find out. She wants you to hang with her and her new crowd on Friday, but you're just not down with it. You know that some of them drink and smoke, and that's just not your bag. You know that your parents would flip if they know you were hanging around with kids like that. Plus, you know that you'll end up breaking curfew and have to sneak into your room through the window like some kind of jewel thief. Now you have to decide if you're going to risk flipping out your 'rents just to hang out with your bud. To make matters worse, you know that if you don't go, your friend will get all upset and hurt that you don't want to hang. It's a sticky situation when emotions are involved. But is it worth it for you? You have to choose.

Sure, you know the difference between right and wrong. It's just crappy that life isn't always that simple. You know that cheating is a big red "wrong." But let's say that your long-time family friend didn't get to study for the social studies test because he had to work at his after-school job and then baby-sit his twin little bros until his mom got off working the late shift. If he flunks, he risks getting kicked off the team, which means no college scholarship. He's really good in social studies anyway and he thinks he knows the material, but he glances over to double-check with your answers. Do you let him? That would be cheating, no doubt about it. "But ... but ...." No buts. As difficult as his situation is, it's still cheating, cut and dried.

Which leads us to another dicey type of situation: being a snitch, a tattletale, a *rat*. Nobody likes a rat. So how are you to handle knowing that someone is getting away with doing something wrong? Whether we're talking lying, stealing, or even intentionally starting a rumor, it's difficult to decide how to handle someone you know is guilty. And if you're friends with the person, it makes it all the more difficult.

Keepin' It Real

"Someone was spraying graffiti on the walls at school and they couldn't catch him. I saw the kid do it one time. I didn't like him, but I still felt weird about telling on him. Pretty soon I told a teacher anyway. I felt weirder not saying anything."

—Kelly, age 14

An added complication is the conflicting influence we feel from outside forces and from inside ourselves: pressure to be accepted, to be liked, to be cool, to rebel. You may not be sure that you want to always do what's expected of you or what's "right." If your parents are road-tripping to Granny's for the weekend, you may be very tempted to throw a raging party at the house. You would get some major cool points from the popular kids at school, it would be a "bad" thing to do, and sometimes you like to be "bad." Plus, it would probably be a lot of fun. Well, before you buy a leather jacket and start calling yourself "Rebel," consider the potential consequences and weigh your options. Is having a party worth getting grounded and having your allowance docked until the next millennium? Is it worth risking stuff getting broken and the house getting trashed? And are you willing to deal with the worst-case scenario, if the bash gets out of control and someone gets hurt? Gather your info and make a decision.

Life is never simple, and moral decisions are some of the most difficult ones to make. But when in doubt, there is a pretty foolproof mantra you can follow: "Do the right thing." You know the difference between good and bad, right and wrong, legal and illegal. Follow laws and rules; they were made for a reason. Take time to consider them, without discounting the emotions and well-being of others. As a strong, intelligent person, it is your responsibility to take the high road, even at times when you feel you're the only one on it. And don't be surprised if others follow your lead.

The Best You Can Do Is Your Best

Decision making is a tough business. Some people just naturally take to it better than others. Most teens, however, are in that "others" category. To avoid feeling tortured by indecision, some will find what they like and stick to it. Forget about an adventurous spirit, these teens subscribe to the "better safe than sorry" theory. By keeping with stuff that's familiar, they can avoid the decision-making process from here on out, plus avoid the potential hazard of making a bad choice. When your family went to a fancy dinner at the local lobster house for Big Momma's birthday, everyone ordered from the menu, but it was all way too exotic for you. You pleaded with the waiter to have them make you a plain burger instead. It's safe, you know you like it, and who wants to risk ordering something that turns out to be nasty? Like you'd ever go near snails or octopus. Yuck!

Too bad that avoiding decision making isn't always so easy. More often than not, you need to step up to plate and swing, even if you have no idea if you'll even hit the ball, let alone which direction it'll go. With all the decisions you are forced to make each day and throughout life—choices of all shapes, sizes, and end results—how can you possibly always make the right ones? You can't.

The scariest thing about making a decision is that you can never be sure of the outcome. Even with the help of a phone psychic, there's no way to know how things will work out. Fear of the unknown is nothing to scoff at. Not many people out there would be willing to explore a cave without a flashlight or would jump off a bridge with a bungee cord that they're not sure works. And yet, that is what decision making is, to a large extent: a black hole of uncertainty. But you've gotta take that risk.

You can't ignore the future, but you can't predict it, either, so don't even try. When making decisions, there's just no sense in worrying about how big a role your decision will play in your future. This is especially true of the distant future. What seems like a sure thing now may seem ridiculous in a year, and the time you spent worrying about the long-lasting, damaging ramifications of a choice you're making will be totally wasted. Frankly, stuff is rarely as huge as you think, even majorly important issues. Afraid of choosing the wrong college? You can always transfer. Terrified of signing up for a college major you'll end up hating? You can switch programs. So try not to let yourself get totally freaked. It takes a lot to overwhelm a together teen like you.

That's not to say that big decisions should be blown off or taken lightly. They cannot and should not be made quickly or haphazardly. Take your time, as much as you need, and consider the situation thoroughly. Use all the tactics we've taught you to make the most educated decision you possibly can. It's also most important to make the choice you want to make, without getting pushed into anything by anybody. If you feel yourself getting wigged out, try visualizing that "worst-case scenario" thing for a sec. Think it out, make your pick, and be confident in the fact that you did the best you could. No dart-throwing decision making in these here parts, no sirree.

Decisions are yours to make, and you need to beware of anyone who tries to force you into anything. But don't confuse that type of interference with getting positive help from the outside. Don't be afraid to ask for advice. Sometimes when you've spent so long considering a situation, you get too close to it and can't see it clearly anymore. But don't go asking just anyone on the street for an opinion. Think about people you know whose ideas you admire and opinions you trust. And think about who knows you best and is maybe even familiar with your situation. Then sit down and talk it out. Explain the state of affairs, and then your thoughts on each of the possible choices. Another person's take on the matter may confirm or disprove what you've already considered and help you make a good choice—or at least narrow down the options.

Then get ready: Once in a while, you will end up making the wrong decision. It's sad, it's frustrating, but it happens, sometimes even after painstakingly careful deliberation. You can't always be perfect, and lots of times when things go wrong, it's totally not your fault. Don't blame yourself. For whatever reason, you'll choose lots of wrong roads in your life, but don't sweat it. You will learn from all of them, which could help save you from the same fate in the future.

In some situations when you know you were wrong, you can go back and change your decision. This can be embarrassing or painful. But sometimes admitting you were wrong is better than living with a wrong decision.

Keepin' It Real

"My friend always wanted to run for student council and then finally did. I thought it would look good for college, so I ran, too. It was kind of a mean thing to do because we were running against each other. When I saw how upset she was, I pulled out of it. I was her campaign manager instead."

—Billy, age 16

Unfortunately, sometimes there's no going back. You are forced to deal with a decision that you can't reverse or change, or a problem that is just unsolvable. The only thing to do is try to make the best of it. If you're smart and a little lucky, you can find a way to use this new situation to your advantage. Things may end up better than they would have otherwise. You just never know how it'll work out. Through it all, feel good about yourself. It's a cinch when you know you've done your best.

The Least You Need to Know

- No problem is too big and no situation too complicated to work through. There aren't always easy answers, but there are answers.

- When making a decision, it is best to be as educated on the factors as possible. Consider the consequences of each choice, and then make your pick.

- It's not always easy to decide how to handle a moral dilemma. Situations can get complicated, and the answer isn't always clear. Listen to your conscience.

- No matter how hard you try, you can't always make the right decision. Learn to live with the new situation, and be confident that you did your best.

Chapter 11

Zen and the Art of Attitude Adjustment

In This Chapter

- Flappin' your gums
- A laugh a day keeps the doctor away
- Inner peace and quiet
- Just chillin'
- Keep away from quicksand

When high stress levels are getting you down, you need to find an escape—and fast! Since you can't beam yourself up to the mothership, you need to find ways to cope with your problems right here and now. By learning how to share your feelings with others and make quality time for yourself, it's possible to regain control of runaway stress. In this chapter, we'll show you some great ways to regroup, recharge, and basically ease your worried mind.

Talk Is Cheap but Priceless

When the going gets tough, what's a teen to do? When school gets to be too much; your steady love breaks up with you; and Cuddles, your pet tarantula, dies, is your first instinct to run and hide, or is it to send out an SOS? People usually handle problems in their lives in one of two ways. Some run to their rooms with a pint of rocky road ice cream, watch hours and hours of cheesy 1980s movies, and insist that they aren't coming out until graduation. Others see the slightest blip on their disaster screens and get right on the phone to blab their problems to anyone who'll listen. They'll talk and talk and talk, weighing every possible solution and outcome. Hours later, they'll collapse on their beds with a pint of rocky road and the remote control, watching hours and hours of cheesy 1980s movies.

What's the difference between these two scenarios? The teens who talked their heads off and vented their feelings are more likely to sleep well that night and wake up with new and improved attitudes. Getting your feelings off your chest helps clear your mind, enabling you to put that set of problems behind you and face a new day. Whether anything is actually resolved during your confab is less important. Just bringing worries or insecurities out into the open allows you to examine them from all sides and really get a sense of the issues at hand. If you are able to discuss the serious matters in your life with friends or family members, you are already hip to a great stress-busting tool.

Keepin' It Real

"I tell my best friend everything! We talk like 20 times a day, from morning 'til night. We can vent about anything, and it really helps."

—Lisa, age 15

People who pull the covers over their heads and hope that messy situations will disappear by the time they come out of hiding are actually inviting the bad feelings to stick around. It's understandable to be nervous about letting all your deepest, darkest emotions out of the closet. Some personal stuff can be embarrassing, and it's scary to think that people won't get it—or, worse yet, will make fun of you for it. But keeping things that bother you to yourself is detrimental to that positive outlook on life and yourself that we told you was so important.

Being an aloof, complicated, loner type might have worked for the guys in those old cowboy movies, but nowadays that character is a little outdated. Despite what the movies tell us, keeping your feelings all bottled up doesn't work for anyone. Modern heroes are more of the touchy-feely variety. Like all the TV talk shows insist, getting in touch with your feelings and exploring your emotions are totally progressive approaches to self-help. Even if it seems corny to you, check in with yourself every once in a while and make sure you're doing okay.

Our emotions need an outlet, and if they have nowhere to go, they can clog up our system. Not literally, of course, but when stuff backs up on you, you start to lose your perspective and clarity on things. When something's on your mind 24/7, your concentration breaks down and your focus falters.

Fighting the Funk

When the chips are down, speak up. Sharing your feelings with trusted friends or family members eases your tension by giving you an outlet to release frustration and doubt.

Everybody needs to be able to lean on at least one good friend or family member when times are tough. As a teen, it's impossible for you to have all the answers to life's big dilemmas. Remember, you're new at a lot of this stuff, and you won't always get it right on the first try. Find someone you trust, and let that person into your world. No one will think you are uncool for venting your frustrations or sharing your fears.

Be wary of being a Negative Nancy. Keep a check on your ranting. The whole world doesn't actually stop when you are in the middle of a personal crisis. Life goes on, and not everybody agrees that your disastrous date Friday night is equal in urgency to resolving the national debt. Talking about your problems is one thing. Talking about nothing *but* your problems is another. Once you've vented, let it go, even if your friends don't react the way you'd hoped they would. Either take your problems to someone else to mull over, or cut your losses and move on.

Unfortunately, we can all be a little selfish and self-involved some-times. If your normal partners in crime are less than interested in hearing about your home hair-highlighting debacle, don't harass them into caring. The kind of advice and support you have to force out of people is not the kind you want. If you can deal with the situation at hand on your own this time, go ahead. However, if you feel that you really need help and your peeps are too wrapped up in their own lives to participate in yours, take it to the next level, as in Mom, your big sis, or Oscar, the pool guy. Don't let your friends' indifference to your troubles make you feel worse about things. Your problems might not be earth-shattering to others, but they are to you, and that means you deserve help with solving them.

Lighten Up!

One of the best remedies for pulling yourself out of a slump is forc-ing yourself to have a good time. At moments when it seems like the hardest thing to do, laughing can be the best blues-buster around. You can't help but feel better after a good, hearty belly laugh. It's scientifically proven.

It's easier to laugh in the face of distress when you already have a decent sense of humor. Being able to chuckle at the disasters that happen on a daily basis is the only way to make them seem less dev-astating. Walking around until third period with the back of your skirt tucked into your tights because you were in such a hurry to get dressed this morning might make some gals transfer to another state. But if you are able to laugh at the hideousness of it all (and the fact that you're now stuck with the nickname "Breezy Betty)," you will be much better at getting a grip after the fact. You can't help that some mortifying stuff is going to happen to you in life, so be prepared to take it in stride; it will all go down a lot smoother.

Being funny and making other people laugh can get you out of a lot of hairy situations, too. A couple of well-placed jokes lightens everyone's mood and puts people at ease. Even old Mrs. Craggenpuss, who seems to enjoy publicly humiliating people, likes to let off some steam every once in a while. So practice your comedy routine in front of the mirror and then let it fly. You'll be the guy everyone wants to have around.

To use an old cliché, laughter is the best medicine. So when you are feeling low, grab some friends and go see a good comedy at the multiplex. See three. Whatever it takes to crack you up. Watching funny movies or TV and hanging out with friends who are fun gets your mind off your troubles. And the joking and laughing you do help lift your spirits and boosts your mental state. An overall state of happiness gives you a super nonstick personality that stress will slide right off of.

Soul Food

We already mentioned how good physical activity can be in helping manage the effects of stress, but there are also mental exercises you can do to calm your nerves. When too many frantic days strike in a row or when you get hit with bad news or a real doozy of an issue, it's more important than ever to take a moment and clear your mind. There are a bunch of different ways to get some kind of inner peace going on when the world is raging outside your door.

Yoga is a great way to take five after a nutty week. Yoga is a type of exercise that combines slow physical movements, like stretching, with deep and controlled breathing. It's great for increasing your flexibility and improving strength, but it's also a terrific way to center yourself mentally. Lots of people keep their eyes closed when they do yoga and make it a point to not talk to anyone else. And you don't have to be an expert yogi to start reaping the rewards; even beginners find it extremely relaxing. Lots of people become die-hard fans, hooked on the great way it makes them feel. Because of the specific way you breathe when you're doing it, yoga slows down your heart rate and blood pressure and balances your internal organs. How's that for a stress-buster? The great thing about yoga is that it can be done anywhere. Once you become familiar with the basic positions, you can do it at home by yourself, on vacation, or wherever and whenever the urge hits you.

Keepin' It Real

"Yoga is very cool because it totally calms you down. I couldn't find a class near me, so I just got one of those how-to videotapes and I loved it. My friends would tease me that it isn't real exercise, but my arms got really buff from doing it a few times a week."

—Kara, 16

Aside from yoga, deep, slow, focused breathing diffuses the effects of panic, anxiety, and anger. It's a great way to let off steam even if you don't have much time. The point is to shift your focus off whatever is stressing you out so that your body can come back into balance.

Here's an exercise that you can do when you're on the go: Put your hand on your diaphragm (that's right under your ribcage) and take a deep breath through your nose. Visualize the air filling your body, pushing your diaphragm and abdomen out. Hold your breath for a slow count of five, and then slowly release all your breath and visualize the air emptying from your body. Pause and relax as you feel your lungs empty completely. Focus on the quiet feeling just before your natural urge to inhale again. Ta da! Instant relaxation.

Meditation is another way to spend time by yourself, quietly clearing your mind of the busy thoughts of the day. It can also include controlled breathing techniques, but it doesn't have to. People who meditate usually pick a certain time of day, like early morning, and a specific place to unwind. You can meditate for 10 minutes or an hour, depending on how much time you have and how stressed you are feeling. You can either play soft music or just listen to the sounds around you (preferably not car horns or fighting neighbors). Some people combine meditation and praying, although you don't have to be religious to meditate.

Spirituality, however, does play a big part in many people's lives and helps them feel more balanced and secure. Having faith in a higher power and an understanding and belief in the teachings of your religion, no matter what it is, can be very comforting in a world that often feels out of control. People who share your beliefs understand where you're coming from and can be good to confide in. Clergy, rabbis, and other spiritual leaders welcome anyone who is feeling confused or lost.

Just Relax

The great thing about relaxation is that there are lots of ways to do it. Different techniques work better depending on how stressed you are and, of course, where you are. Sometimes it's just not appropriate to kick off your shoes, close your eyes, and chant.

If you just need some down time after finals week or a big game, relaxation is easy to come by. For example, cranking up your stereo and rocking out to your favorite tunes is a great way to let off steam. Grab a stack of magazines or that new book you've been dying to read, and head to the beach. Turn off your pager and your cell phone. Taking the time to "chill out" either by yourself or with close friends will do wonders for your stressed-out state of mind.

With hectic schedules and on-the-go lifestyles, it's easy to forget how important alone time is. Allowing yourself the freedom to do the things you want, not just the things everyone expects you to do, is really important. Find the time to explore hobbies that interest you, not just the things that you think will look good on paper.

Participating in activities that are distracting, like playing games or sports, playing an instrument, or even shopping, are great ways to temporarily get your mind off your troubles. Sometimes all you need is a break in the day to recharge your batteries. Later, when you turn your attention back to the problems at hand, you'll have a clearer head and a better perspective on how to tackle them.

Keepin' It Real

"My favorite thing to do on a Saturday night or something is to have my three best friends come over and bake a whole batch of cookies. Then we eat them and watch movies all night long."

—Stacey, age 13

Even though you get busted when you do this in class, spacing out or daydreaming can actually be good for you. Let your mind wander for a while. Picture yourself lying in the sun by a great big pool while an adorable waitperson brings you a juicy cheeseburger. Mmmm. Or, wait. Imagine yourself accepting an Academy Award, thanking all of your friends and the "little people" who helped you get where you are today. Oops. Where were you? It may seem silly and frivolous, but who cares? You're allowed to be silly—you're imagining it.

These are all general things you can do to keep your spirits up whenever you need a boost. Sometimes, though, you need immediate help in combating the toughies that pop up. When stress hits hard, you need to relax—and you need to relax now!

If you can—hit the pavement. In a moment of extreme stress, panic, or anxiety, take a hike. Literally. Get moving with a brisk walk or jog. It will do wonders for you. Do whatever you can to get moving—kickbox, ride a bike, skateboard, whatever. Remember, the activity gets rid of some of those stress chemicals that can build up when we can't "fight or flee."

Certain relaxation exercises also instantly reduce stress by having you tense and then relax specific muscles or body parts. When you're feeling crunched, think about the parts of you that are getting hit the hardest (like your back and neck). Then think of other specific areas of your body, like your hands and arms; your feet and lower legs; your thighs and butt; your abdomen, chest, shoulders, neck, jaw, and lower face; and your upper face and forehead. Tense each area and hold for a count of 5, and then relax completely. If you have the time, you can use this method on every major area of your body. And, boy, will you feel like a new person! At first, you might make some really funny faces, but when you get really good, you can actually do it in public and no one will be able to tell!

Privacy is a big deal to most teens, so we get that you don't really want to announce your frustrations by doing a sun salutation in homeroom. But some stress relievers you can keep under wraps, like keeping a journal. Writing down your thoughts can help unravel a difficult problem right before your eyes. We can get so overwhelmed by the events of the day that by the end of it, we feel like bursting into tears and aren't even sure why. Taking the time to write things down means that you will not only be engaging in some much-needed quiet time, but you'll also be reliving the moments of your day. By going over events in your head, it's easier to see the real story, not just how you perceived things to be. A conversation that was monumental earlier might seem less so in retrospect.

Beware of Burnout

Learning how to relax is key in beating the short- and long-term effects of stress, and there are lots of fast and fun ways to do it. Making "fun time" a priority in your life is a sure-fire way to beat burnout.

Find inspiration in other people you admire. Lots of historical figures, celebrities, and sports heroes have interesting personal stories. It always helps to read about people who overcame hardships and obstacles and became really successful despite it all. Maybe you know of someone famous who is from your hometown or who had a rough childhood. Learning about other people's experiences not only can put your life and problems in perspective, but it also can show you that you don't have to be trapped by your current situation or circumstance.

Sometimes you can find inspiration right in your own backyard. Maybe you have a favorite uncle whose hobby of restoring old cars makes him one of the coolest guys you know. Or your grandpa, the war hero, loves to reminisce about the old days. Ask him about how he earned his medals. People close to you who have lived a little often have great stories to pass on and give even greater advice.

Unnecessary Evils

Whatever you choose to do to unwind or relax is fine, as long as it really works. Since no two people's problems or personalities are the same, there are no hard-and-fast rules when it comes to kicking back. However, there are a few traps to avoid when trying to beat the heat.

Trying to take the easy way out of anything almost always guarantees that you will shortchange yourself. Looking for a quick fix to problems will give you only temporary solutions. People think that drinking and smoking cigarettes "takes the edge off" of a bad day. No matter what anyone tells you, these things are not true stress relievers. Alcohol can make you feel relaxed at first, but it also makes you woozy, bloated, and dehydrated. And let's not forget those nasty hangovers the next day. A hangover feels like you've been hit over the head with a sledgehammer and like someone laid carpet on your tongue. Yuck.

Smoking actually makes your heart beat faster because nicotine, the main ingredient in cigarettes, is a stimulant. It can also make you jittery, like after you drink a cup of coffee. Great, just what you needed. Smoking can also make you smell bad, turn your teeth yellow, and give you premature wrinkles. Sexy.

And though totally less tragic, watching loads of TV or having movie marathons when your college applications are stacking up so high that you can't open your closet door anymore is not relaxation. It's denial. If you've got real issues to address, playing video games or chatting online only makes matters worse. Don't avoid work that needs to get done. Procrastination is not relaxation's friendly big sister. It's an evil cousin. Know the difference, and plan accordingly.

Although the urge to get lost in these kinds of activities can be strong, remember that they are not going to benefit you. Procrastination usually adds to your stress by making you feel even more backed against a wall as your deadlines loom and your work piles up. It's okay to take a break for an hour in the middle of a major study session as long as you go back to the books when your hiatus is over.

The Least You Need to Know

- Even if you don't come up with solutions, sharing your feelings with others often makes you feel like a burden has been lifted from your shoulders.

- Keeping your spirits up is a great weapon against stress. Find everyday ways to keep humor and laughter a regular part of your life.

- A peaceful mind and body will give you a terrific shield against overwhelming stress. Calming yourself from within is possible through many types of exercise and spiritual exploration.

- It's really important to make the most of your free time. Use it to do the activities you enjoy, and hang out with people who make you feel good about yourself.

Chapter 12

Success Through Stress

In This Chapter

- Making stress work for you
- The buddy system
- The sky's the limit
- It's not easy, it's life

Even though life can be like an amusement park ride that you desperately want to get off, you're stuck holding on for dear life. The combination of constant struggles, ups and downs, and the outside frustrations of modern living can put some major wear and tear on your mind and your body. But hope for survival is just around the corner. You have the power to turn a bad situation around. In this chapter, we'll show you how to make stress work *for* you, not *against* you.

Turning Stress Around

Remember, by definition, stress is not necessarily negative. It is simply the body's reaction to any kind of change in the environment. It just so happens that you go through so many changes daily that it can feel like your insides are dancing a jig. But you can actually fight adversity head on by taking charge of your life. You can grab stress by the throat, throw it against the wall, and say, "Now listen here. You and I are going to work together, understand?" Of course, stress won't answer you back, but, just like dealing with your little brother, you don't have to wait for a response before you go about your business. Take control now by drawing strong boundaries for what you will or won't let get you down and what kind of treatment you will accept from others.

Boundaries are rules that you make for yourself that other people must follow to a certain extent, if they want to be friends with you. Earlier we talked about how to not let yourself be taken advantage of by people in your life, like how it's not okay for your friends to expect you to chauffeur them around every weekend. It's not okay for a bully at school to push you around and take your stuff, and it's not okay to let your peers pressure you into doing something that you don't want to, like having sex or doing drugs. If you know in your head what's acceptable behavior for you, you'll know how to draw the line when you're asked to participate in activities that you aren't into. Saying "no" will come automatically. You shouldn't be made to feel uncomfortable about your decisions, and you won't if you maintain the all-important element of control.

Fighting the Funk

Beat the blahs by showing stress who's boss. Use your powers of positive thinking to turn negative situations around.

It may sound crazy, but you should be grateful for some of the stress in your life. We aren't advocating keeping your life filled with tension, but it is possible to have a healthy amount of stress going on. To a certain degree, stress does have positive qualities. It keeps you motivated, pushes you to go further, and helps you strive for better things in life. Pressure to succeed is not the worst thing in the world if it helps you reach your goals. Often people really excel when they're on the clock. Pressure forces you to learn skills like time management, efficiency, and prioritizing, which are fabulous things to stock up on for your travels down the road of life.

Too little stress in your life can bring on the blahs. If you never feel antsy or rushed by anything, chances are good that you also don't feel energized or inspired. Too little pressure in life can make you lazy and bored. The term "slacker" didn't come from nowhere. It's not just about the baggy flannel shirt and dirty hair. A slacker attitude is a general approach to life that's all about avoiding some of the best parts of it. By rejecting school or work, you're giving up on some potentially really fulfilling experiences—and ones that could affect your future. It's not cool or constructive in any way.

Keepin' It Real

"When I first moved to this town, I hardly did anything in school because I felt so weird about being the new kid. I basically just sat on my couch for that whole first year, totally bored and out of it. I was too freaked out to join the band like I wanted to because I thought I might not be as good as everyone else. I finally forced myself to audition, and this year I had five solos."

—Kevin, age 16

That's why it's so important to try to create a balance in your life, having just the right amount of stress around to help keep you on your toes. You can start doing this by recognizing the greatest sources of your stress—in other words, where it's coming from the most. Are your impending college application deadlines making you queasy? Are you terrified that your date will ask you to sleep with him on prom night? Are your parents going through a messy divorce? By pinpointing what's eating at you, you can begin to tackle it logically.

If it's your applications, then clear some space in your schedule, park yourself in a quiet place, pick one up, and have a go at it. The idea of something is often much more intimidating than actually doing it. If you're indecisive about sex, take the time to really think about it so that you know what you'll do when faced with the situation. If you know but are afraid that it's the unpopular choice, tell whoever needs to know before prom night. Get that conversation out of the way so that you can enjoy yourself.

If it's trouble at home that you're having, sit your parents down and give them a good talking to. Turn the tables and boss them around for once. Let them know that their woes are bringing you down and that it's not fair. They need to deal with their issues, and you need to get on with your life. You have the strength to solve major problems, so exercise it.

In the worst-case scenarios when the issues seem really negative or overwhelming, the best thing you can do is try to dig up that old silver lining. Have you been rejected from more colleges than you thought you'd be? Fewer choices will make your final decision a lot easier to make. If your date breaks up with you because you said you weren't ready to do "it" on prom night, at least you know now. It sure beats having a post-buffet blowout that ends up with you making a horrifying exit with everyone watching. Now that would be bad.

You'll get the hang of it. Use these tactics a few times, and it will start to get easier. Pretty soon you'll be able to put a positive spin on the ugliest of scenarios.

A Friend in Deed

In high school, your friends mean everything to you. Besides defining your clique of comrades, your friends are a major lifeline throughout your teen years. You rely on them for everything from expert fashion advice to midnight chats over your sorry love life. Your closest friends are the ones you know you can count on through thick and thin. These relationships are priceless.

A good friend is one who gives support unconditionally. A good friend will tell you that you look like a supermodel even though you're only 5 foot 2, who calls you a genius when you fail chemistry, and who insists they he is not embarrassed when Dad drives you to the party at that cute upperclassman's house in his old station wagon.

A good friend will lend you her best shoes for that hot date or his car to drive across state lines to visit that amazing girl you met at camp and will let you stay at her house for a week when your parents have one of their awful fighting bouts. Hold fast to this friendship because it truly can save your life.

Keepin' It Real

"Last year I broke my leg playing softball. I was out of school for months and was so depressed because I felt like I was missing out on all these really fun things that everyone else was doing. My best friend, Jen, came and sat with me in the hospital every day after school and then after I went home. I swear, I would not have gotten through that without her."

—Katie, age 15

Because of all that friends can offer, it's important to learn how to pick good ones. When you're young, it's much easier to bond with other people over superficial things. But as you get older and smarter, you also become choosier. Your friends need to not only share your taste in music and clothes, but also to understand who you are and where you're coming from. It's nice to hook up with people who have common experiences, similar backgrounds, or shared goals. These can be really important factors in forming an attachment to someone. Linking with people who share your values and beliefs will be the most rewarding kinds of relationships, either friendly or romantic, because they will be the most fulfilling.

It's hard to be good friends with people who weren't raised to treat people the way you were or who don't have strong personalities and morals. Hold your ground when picking your friends. Remember, these are the people you need to be able to trust with your most private secrets and emotions. Don't be wishy-washy or feel compelled to just hang out with the cool kids if they aren't really all that.

And the same goes for picking boyfriends and girlfriends. These relationships are also super-important because you want to develop a closeness with these folks that is different from your friends. It is a very mature kind of relationship, but if you are ready to have it, just make sure that you do it with care. Be with someone who appreciates who you are and supports the things you believe in, even if it is different from what she is into. People can be different; we all just have to respect those differences.

Lots of people have gotten flack over the person they chose to go out with. Depending on where you live, what religion you practice, or your parents' value system, relationships can really spark some fire. If you truly care about someone, don't succumb to pressure from others to break it off—especially if it's just because of the way someone looks, her clothes, or the people she hangs out with. You wouldn't want someone to reject you based on these superficial things, so don't be guilty of it yourself.

It's also really important that this person respect you. Going out with someone who treats you badly is an automatic no-no. It doesn't matter how cool or smart or cute that person is. If he talks down to you, ignores you, makes fun of you, or simply doesn't respect you and the boundaries you've set for yourself, he isn't worth keeping around. You are better than that.

If you don't already do so, learn to lean on your good, trustworthy friends. Talk to them about what's going on in your head, take their advice, and let them help you out when you need it. And don't forget to be a good friend back. Knowing how to give as good as you get is crucial for building long and healthy relationships.

If you know someone who is troubled, help out by showing some compassion. This would not be the time to comment on how he always overreacts or has annoying mood swings. Be supportive by acknowledging what he is going through and offering to go through it with him. Remind him of his positive qualities and strengths, and why you are friends with him in the first place. And if it's your friend who runs out on prom night because her date called her a loser for not wanting to have sex, that means it's time to say your goodbyes, too. Respond to the call of duty with a hanky and a little moral support.

If your friend's problems are more serious or severe or if you just feel overwhelmed and unequipped to deal with them, say so. Tell your friend this, and suggest that she get help from either a parent or a counselor. Sometimes people's problems are bigger than they are, and they need professional help to deal with them the right ways. There is no shame in this, nor are you a bad or incompetent friend because you couldn't fix things.

Having positive relationships can really affect the quality of your life not just now, but forever. Having a good support system and people you can rely on gives a person a great sense of comfort and stability. It makes the tough times easier to ride out when you know that you aren't facing them alone. Make your relationships, whether romantic or platonic, a priority in your life. Be the best friend you can be.

Beware of Burnout

Learn to nurture your friendships. A trusted confidant is a jewel more valuable than diamonds. So if you're lucky enough to have one, use him. Rely on your friends to pull you through the hard items, and always remember to return the favor.

Shoot for the Moon

With a new attitude toward stress and a new lease on life, you're ready to take on the world. With your confidence and self-esteem in check, you're a fearless flyer, ready to show off what you're made of. Don't hold back—now is your time to shine.

It's not that you *have* anything to prove; it's that you have something you *want* to prove. Proving to yourself and others that you can accomplish things does wonders for your self-esteem and gives you the confidence to aim even higher. To help raise the bar, it's okay to engage in a little healthy competition. Pitting yourself against others you admire or who you think set high standards for themselves is a good way to make yourself rise to the occasion. See how you measure up against others, and then strive to do even better the next time. But doing something aggressively just to beat someone else or make them feel bad is not the goal. Achievements made out of mean-spiritedness, jealousy, or spite are not as fulfilling or commendable. The means to your end count, and foul play is not rewarding and is rarely justified.

Keepin' It Real

"I was scared to apply to this special high school because it meant going through a ton of scary interviews. I was terrified, but I really wanted to go there. So I sent in an application. I practiced interviewing for, like, months with my mom. Even though I was nervous and shaking, I went in and did it, and they accepted me."

—Lisa, age 14

You succeed in life not only by being true to yourself, but also by being willing to take chances. Risk is a big part of life, and it's important to differentiate between those that are likely to have a big pay-off and those that are more likely to sink you faster than the Titanic. Learning to take advantage of unexpected opportunities is a fantastic way to get the most of out of life and what the world has to offer. Look for ways to shake things up and be different from the norm. We're not talking skydiving with a parachute here; we're talking planning a day trip or breaking up with someone who's holding you back. These are good risks to take. Once you get a feel for appropriate risk taking, don't be afraid to jump right in and grab onto life.

Staying Strong

Regardless of how practiced you become, risk taking won't always work in your favor. Be prepared for that, too. When things don't go your way, don't be too hard on yourself about it. Life is full of honest mistakes and even failure. Falling short on something that you went out on a limb to try is still a huge accomplishment in its own right. After all, you put yourself out there. Just don't let yourself be discouraged by defeat. Some of the brainiest and most successful people in the world messed things up the first 20 times they tried. But they went for a twenty-first time. All it takes is one success to change your life for the better.

Life will throw you continuous curveballs, and it's up to you to keep up. As you get older, your problems will become bigger. Even though it seems like your current problems are monumental and you couldn't imagine anything worse, believe us, they're out there. The thing is, life just gets more complicated—for everybody. After college comes choosing a career, getting your first job, and dealing with all the stress and pressures that come with being in the working world. Then comes the decision to have a family of your own, where to live, and so on and so on.

Your personal relationships will change, too, not only becoming more intense, but also shifting as you do. As you grow and change, the type of person you are attracted to will as well. As we age, we look for different qualities in people than we did as teens, and as we develop our careers and hobbies, the available room in our lives for free time and personal endeavors shrinks. As a result, the people you will want to spend that time with need to be of quality. You aren't going to want or need people around who suck you dry or wear you out. You want to hang with people who are fun, who offer their support, and who are as ambitious and driven as you are. Having these types of people in your life, including your family, will really help fill in the cracks when the world's challenges hit your foundation hard.

That's why developing a solid foundation now will help you tremendously in dealing with personal and professional experiences down the road. The rest of life is a lot like high school, so if you can master that, there's a good chance that you won't succumb to the nastiness of the real world. You've heard your parents complain about their everyday trials and tribulations. And it's not just because they're your parents, the people who get lost on the way to the mall. We all will have to deal with mean bosses, broken hearts, and the deaths of loved ones. They are inevitable occurrences in every person's life. But how you choose to deal with these things will determine whether you are defeated by it all or whether you learn and grow from adversity.

Controlling the elements in your life that you do have power over, and learning how to take the things that you don't control in stride, can change the state of your entire world. Learning to rise above the bad and concentrate on the good will give you the greatest potential for a happy life.

And remember that your opinion of yourself counts for a lot. Stand tall, believe in who you are and what you can accomplish, and the odds will be in your favor that you will make all your dreams come true.

The Least You Need to Know

- Remember that not all stress is bad. You can turn almost any situation around so that it works in your favor.

- Learn to use your friends as a means of support, and make yourself available to others when they are in need of help.

- When you see other people succeed, try to be happy for them. Use their accomplishments as an opportunity to ask how you can improve yourself.

- Now that you're equipped with lots of stress-busting knowledge, use what you've learned to keep calm while you conquer the world!

Check out other *Complete Idiot's Guide® for Teens* Books

SPIRITUALITY

The Complete Idiot's Guide®
to Spirituality for Teens
ISBN: 002863926X

DATING

**The Complete Idiot's Guide®
to Dating for Teens
ISBN:** 0028639995

LOOKING GREAT

The Complete Idiot's Guide®
to Looking Great for Teens
ISBN: 0028639855

ALPHA